WHATEVER HAPPENS

OTHER BOOKS BY ROBERT MORGAN

Calm Your Anxiety

The 50 Final Events in World History

A Song in My Heart

Great Is Thy Faithfulness

The Jordan River Rules

100 Bible Verses That Made America

Reclaiming the Lost Art of Biblical Meditation

The Strength You Need

Mastering Life Before It's Too Late

The Red Sea Rules

Then Sings My Soul

WHATEVER HAPPENS

HOW TO STAND FIRM
in YOUR FAITH When the
WORLD Is FALLING APART

Robert J. Morgan

W PUBLISHING GROUP

AN IMPRINT OF THOMAS NELSON

ISBN 978-0-7852-5393-8 (audiobook)
ISBN 978-0-7852-5392-1 (eBook)
ISBN 978-0-7852-5390-7 (HC)

Library of Congress Control Number: 2023946261

Printed in the United States of America

23 24 25 26 27 LBC 5 4 3 2 1

To Luke

CONTENTS

INTRODUCTION

Whatever happens, conduct yourselves in a
manner worthy of the gospel of Christ.

PHILIPPIANS 1:27

The *Washington Post* recently asked readers to describe today's world in a single word. Some of the answers were unfit for a family newspaper, but the top three printable responses were: Exhausting. Lost. Chaotic.[1]

Who doesn't feel that way?

Sometimes I feel exhausted, lost, and chaotic too. Don't you?

What can we do about it? Thanks for joining me on this trip (and back in time) to revisit the ancient church of the Philippians. No passport needed.

We've landed in northeastern Greece, where we've entered a lovely villa belonging to a member of the local church. People are gathering quickly because news has spread that a letter has arrived. A traveling church member has returned from Rome, where he saw the imprisoned apostle Paul. The traveler brought precious cargo—what we know as the epistle to the Philippians.

We take our seats with other Christ followers as the pastor calls the service to order. We see with a glance the letter isn't long. A couple pieces of parchment, which the pastor unrolls and begins to read. He speaks loudly so no one misses a word.

"Paul and Timothy, servants of Christ Jesus, to all God's holy people in

Christ Jesus at Philippi." That's you, that's me. We've put ourselves in the picture. As we listen, we realize afresh that even the most prominent missionary in New Testament history lived with uncertainty.

Paul wrote phrases like: "what has happened to me" (Philippians 1:12); "what has happened to me will turn out" (1:19); "whatever happens, conduct yourselves in a manner worthy of the gospel" (1:27); "as soon as I find out what is going to happen to me" (2:23 NLT); "whatever happens" (3:1 NLT); and "whatever the circumstances" (4:11).

Whatever. Whatever happens. The apostle Paul was facing uncharted circumstances and an unsettled future. He didn't know if he would be released or executed. He didn't know if he would live or die. But he knew one thing: Whatever happened, he was going to stand firm in the faith and conduct himself in a manner worthy of the gospel.

So must we. You and I are living in unpredictable days, and no one knows what will happen to our world, our nation, or our families from day to day. This uncertainty leaves so many exhausted, lost, in chaos.

But not us. We should be standing firm in the Holy Spirit (1:27); having the mind of Christ (2:5); being children of God in a warped generation (2:15); pressing toward the upward goal (3:14); acting like citizens of heaven (3:20); practicing joy (4:4); turning problems into prayer (4:6); having a peace that transcends understanding (4:7); learning to be content whatever the circumstances (4:11); and knowing God will meet all our needs according to the riches of His glory (4:19).

That's the message of Philippians.

Every verse reminds us to keep ourselves together in a world that's falling apart because we have a Savior who gives us the strength to do all things through Him (4:13). Even as the globe unravels, we can stay unruffled.

Philippians is one of the most practical books of the Bible. I've been teaching and preaching from its four chapters for half a century, yet its message to me is ever fresh. Its theme is summed up in these words: "Whatever happens, conduct yourselves in a manner worthy of the gospel of Christ. . . . Stand firm . . . without being frightened in any way by those who oppose you" (1:27–28).

We can trust our unchanging God with the uncertainties of today, tomorrow, and beyond as we hold firmly to the truth in a world that's hanging by a thread.

It's high time we did that because the world isn't likely to get better before Christ comes. And until that happens, He wants His children to live with relentless courage and irrepressible joy, just as Paul told the Philippians to do.

I first presented these chapters as episodes on my Bible study podcast—*The Robert J. Morgan Podcast*. Now, with heavenly help, I've converted them into thirty-one short chapters to encourage you to remember, though the times are uncertain, that God's truth is unfailing.

In the following pages, let's linger awhile in our Philippian villa and ponder every word of the letter that was first read there—crafted by Paul, inspired by God, highly useful, written for us, giving critical directions for these critical times. The letter to the Philippians will show us what to do, whatever happens in this world.

For a ten-part study guide and video series based on this book, visit robertjmorgan .com.

Chapter 1

WHATEVER HAPPENS . . .

TRUST GOD'S GUIDANCE WHEN PERPLEXED

(ACTS 16:6-10)

I grew up in Carter County, Tennessee, and I still have a home alongside the Appalachian Trail at the base of Roan Mountain, which, at its highest ridge, towers 6,200 feet above sea level. There's speculation about how the Roan got its name. A likely explanation comes from its rhododendron bushes. On its heights grow the largest natural rhododendron gardens on earth.

But my father, who grew up there, told me the Roan was named for Daniel Boone's horse. Boone was exploring the area on a roan-patterned horse in the late 1700s or early 1800s when the animal became lame. Leaving it there, Boone lost his bearings as he explored the dense terrain on foot.

A year later, Boone visited again and found his horse fat and sleek. He named the mountain for the horse—Roan. Later when asked if he had really gotten lost, Boone replied, "I can't say as ever I was lost, but I was bewildered once for three days."[1]

As I look over my life with its mountains and valleys and summers and winters, I can say I've never totally lost my way, but I've often been bewildered. The paths were not as clear as I expected, and I faced more closed doors than open ones.

The apostle Paul could say the same. He encountered a lot of closed doors, especially on his second missionary journey. Notice the words I've italicized in Acts 16:6–8:

> Paul and his companions traveled throughout the region of Phrygia and Galatia, *having been kept by the Holy Spirit* from preaching the word in the province of Asia. When they came to the border of Mysia, they tried to enter Bithynia, but the *Spirit of Jesus would not allow them to.* So they passed by Mysia and went down to Troas.

Sir William Ramsey, who studied the life of Paul for decades and became a foremost scholar on his travels, said, "This is in many respects the most remarkable paragraph in Acts."[2]

As Paul, Silas, and Timothy pressed east to west across the great expanse of Asia Minor (modern-day Turkey), every door was closed to them, every option forbidden, every opportunity denied. God had sent them on a mission, then closed the doors.

This was perplexing for Paul. There he was, prepared, eager, and on a mission to preach among people who needed the gospel, but the Holy Spirit said, "Don't do it."

Finally they went as far as they could, to the eastern port of Troas. The total distance from their point of origin in Antioch of Syria to Troas, which is on the Aegean Sea, is over a thousand miles. Paul and his companions were trying to follow God's will, but they found one door closed after another for a thousand miles.

Have you ever felt that way?

Things finally changed in Troas. Look at what happened in verses 9–10:

> During the night Paul had a vision of a man of Macedonia standing and begging him, "Come over to Macedonia and help us." After Paul had seen

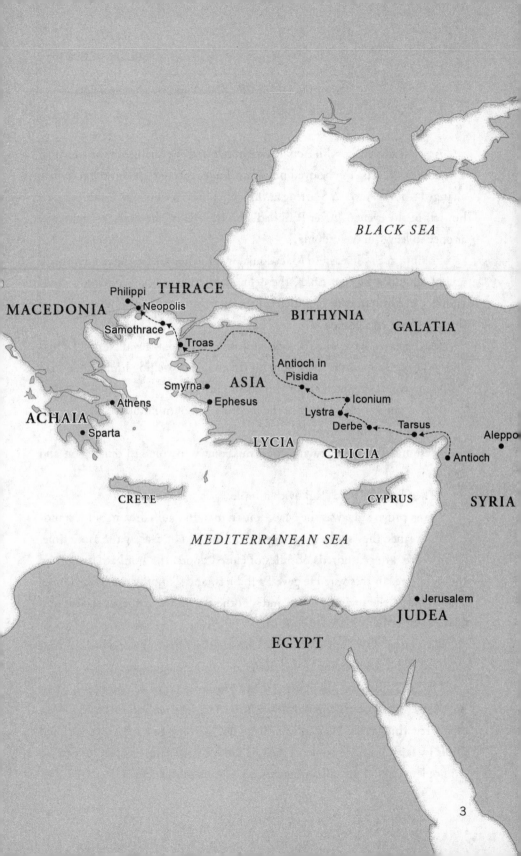

the vision, we got ready at once to leave for Macedonia, concluding that God had called us to preach the gospel to them.

As we read this story in Acts 16, we notice a subtle change in the wording. The author of Acts, the beloved physician Luke, showed up and the narrative changed from *they* to *we*. Starting at this very point in the story, Luke included himself in the events. "After Paul had seen the vision," he said, "*we* got ready at once to leave for Macedonia."

Philippi, a city in eastern Macedonia, was the home of a respected medical school. Could it be that Luke, the beloved physician, was a student or staff member in Philippi who had traveled to Troas for reasons unknown? Was he the man from Macedonia?[3]

Maybe when he awoke the next morning, Paul took a walk around Troas and suddenly spotted the man from his dream. Approaching him, Paul asked, "Who are you? I dreamed about you last night."

"My name is Luke. I'm from the medical school in Philippi."

"Are you a Jesus follower?"

"Yes, and I've been praying for a missionary to come to our region and help us."

"Then let's go," said Paul, with a smile.

I can't prove Luke was the Macedonian man in Paul's dream, but it stands to reason since they showed up together in the text at exactly the same time. In any case, after hundreds of miles of closed doors, the Lord at last opened the right one. In this way He gave Paul, Silas, and Timothy the Macedonian call, added a helper named Luke, and sent them with the gospel westward into Europe rather than eastward into Asia.

That changed the entire sweep of Christian history—of world history. And the Lord did it using many closed doors and a single open one.

Here is a life lesson for all of us. The Lord closes far more doors for us than He opens, for there are thousands of things He does *not* want us to do—but only a few things that He *does* want us to do. We have to bypass all the closed doors by faith until we come to the one God is preparing to open for us. We cannot let closed doors discourage us, for God is in the details.

So God sent Paul to Europe, and his first stop was the city of Philippi. This story has taught me four things about seeking and finding the will of God.

God's Will for Our Lives Is Sometimes Perplexing, So We Walk by Faith

We don't always understand why we feel shut out or encounter closed doors or have to wait for circumstances to change. But part of the reason is that the Lord is teaching us to walk by faith.

WE HAVE TO BYPASS ALL THE CLOSED DOORS BY FAITH UNTIL WE COME TO THE ONE GOD IS PREPARING TO OPEN FOR US. WE CANNOT LET CLOSED DOORS DISCOURAGE US, FOR GOD IS IN THE DETAILS.

When I graduated from Wheaton in 1976, I drove back to Roan Mountain to look for a church to pastor and to prepare for my wedding to Katrina that fall. There were many little churches in the mountains needing a pastor, but none of them wanted to hire me. For the entire first year of our marriage, every door in front of me remained closed. Then, on our first wedding anniversary, a little country church outside Greeneville, Tennessee, sounded a Macedonian call and said, "Come over here and help us." In the years that followed, we were as thankful for the closed doors as we were for the one that opened.

Early in my career as a pastor, I created a little book for parents to use in leading their children to Christ. A friend asked to publish it, so I shook hands on the deal. Shortly afterward, Thomas Nelson Publishers (now part of HarperCollins Christian Publishing) became interested. For an unpublished author to land a contract with a major publisher was a fantastic opportunity. But my friend still wanted to publish the book. I kept my word to him, but he wasn't able to follow through. It was like two doors slammed in my face.

But soon Thomas Nelson suggested another book—and in the decades since, I've had scores of HarperCollins Christian Publishing resources published involving millions of copies. Plus, another publisher took on my original project. I've learned, when perplexed, to trust God. He knows what He is doing. He is in the details.

The German hymn "Now Thank We All Our God" has this beautiful stanza:

> *O may this bounteous God*
> *Through all our life be near us,*
> *With ever joyful hearts*
> *And blessèd peace to cheer us;*
> *And keep us in His grace,*
> *And guide us when perplexed;*
> *And free us from all ills*
> *In this world and the next!*

② God's Will for Our Lives Is Progressive: That's Why We Keep Knocking on Doors

Look at verse 7: "When they came to the border of Mysia, they tried to enter Bithynia, but the Spirit of Jesus would not allow them to." They *tried*. They tried this way and that.

The Lord knew exactly where He wanted them to go. He could have told them from the beginning: "Go straight to Troas where you'll get a Macedonian call." But He didn't. I don't understand why. All I know is that's the way life has worked for me too.

If we're too passive, we never knock on doors. We just wait to see if the Lord will open them without putting forth the necessary effort and risk. If we're too aggressive, we might push the doors open and go where God doesn't intend for us to go.

I've found the best approach is to knock softly or nudge against the door. If it opens, praise the Lord. If it doesn't, praise the Lord, trust His plan, and move on.

THE BEST APPROACH IS TO KNOCK SOFTLY OR NUDGE AGAINST THE DOOR. IF IT OPENS, PRAISE THE LORD. IF IT DOESN'T, PRAISE THE LORD, TRUST HIS PLAN, AND MOVE ON.

God's Will for Our Lives Is Premeditated: That's Why We Stay Positive

The most remarkable thing about this passage—and you have to read it closely or you'll miss it—is the involvement of the Trinity. Though Paul was confused, the entire Godhead—Father, Son, and Holy Spirit—was collaborating to synchronize everything in his future. Paul and his companions were "kept by the Holy Spirit" from preaching in Asia (v. 6), and then Jesus wouldn't let them go to Bithynia (v. 7). Finally, God called them to preach in Macedonia (v. 10).

Do you see it? God the Father called them to preach the gospel in Macedonia. God the Son planned the route. God the Holy Spirit guided them down the unknown path one step at a time.

In the first volume in my series of books called *Then Sings My Soul,* I told the story of how Joseph Gilmore wrote the hymn "He Leadeth Me."[4] Gilmore's father was the governor of New Hampshire during the darkest days of the Civil War. One day, Gilmore was asked to speak at a church in Philadelphia on the Twenty-third Psalm, but he couldn't get past the words, "He leadeth me in the paths of righteousness for his name's sake" (Psalm 23:3 KJV).

Joseph described God's wonderful guidance, even in perplexing times. He later said the words of that verse took hold of him as they had never done before, and after the service he took a blank piece of paper and quickly wrote the words to this hymn.

This song has been a comfort and a blessing to me all of my life. Its words have filtered through my thoughts again recently as I faced a major uncertainty in my life, reminding me: "His faithful follower I would be, for by His hand He leadeth me."[5]

God's Will for Our Lives Is Purposeful: That's Why We Cannot Stop

By the end of the story in Acts 16, Paul and his fellow travelers had made it to Troas, seen the man from Macedonia, met the physician Luke, crossed to modern-day Europe, and brought the gospel to the city of Philippi. They could not, *would not* stop.

At age seventy, I've been looking back over my life, noting the practicality of this strange paragraph in Acts. The doors I really wanted to open didn't. Other doors that I could never have imagined opening did. There have been far more closed doors than open ones for me, because for every one thing the Lord wanted me to do, there were a hundred He didn't.

I didn't realize it then, but I see it now.

We may become bewildered for a few days—as the disciples were on the weekend of Christ's crucifixion. But then Sunday dawned, and clarity came. God uses circumstances to guide us, but the circumstances are always under His control. Don't worry so much about closed doors—just keep praying for the Macedonian call, and God will lead you there.

Whatever happens, know this: Even when you're perplexed, God is orchestrating your footsteps and your future. Just say with the hymn writer: "Your faithful follower I would be, for by Your hand You leadeth me."

Chapter 2

WHATEVER HAPPENS . . .

BUILD YOUR OWN
MENTAL HYMNBOOK

(ACTS 16:11-34)

After Paul's Macedonian call, he and his team booked passage across the Aegean Sea and arrived in Philippi, a wealthy Roman city in Macedonia (modern northeastern Greece) with a vast outdoor theater, broad marketplaces, colonnaded streets, and tons of citizens. Like most Roman cities, it had baths, a gymnasium, a library, and a public latrine (seating three dozen). Nearby were famous gold and gem mines, and the port of Neapolis was only ten miles east on the busy trade route, the Via Egnatia. The population was estimated to have been ten thousand to fifteen thousand people.[1]

Luke reported the story in Acts 16:11–14:

From Troas we put out to sea and sailed . . . to Neapolis. From there we traveled to Philippi, a Roman colony and the leading city of that district of Macedonia. And we stayed there several days. On the Sabbath we went outside the city gate to the river, where we expected to find a place of prayer.

We sat down and began to speak to the women who had gathered there. One of those listening was a woman from the city of Thyatira named Lydia, a dealer in purple cloth.

If we could visit Lydia's booth in the Philippian agora, we would have been wide-eyed at her luxurious fabrics and colors. Her home city of Thyatira was famous for its production of this cloth. Apparently Lydia exported the fabric to Philippi and ran a thriving business. She became Paul's first convert in Europe, and her house became the meeting place for the church that soon formed in this city.

Shortly afterward, another woman was converted—not a wealthy businesswoman but a demonic slave. Her conversion sparked a riot, leading to a physical attack on Paul and Silas. They were stripped and whipped (vv. 16–24). We can only imagine how painful this would be. In the civil rights classic book *Twelve Years a Slave*, Solomon Northup said when he was being whipped, his whole body felt like it was on fire, and he thought he might die. After their beatings, Paul and Silas were placed in stocks with their feet spread apart and their hands restrained, unable to soothe their wounds.

But now we come to one of the most remarkable scenes in the book of Acts, relayed in verses 25 through 34 of chapter 16. "About midnight," we read, "Paul and Silas were praying and singing hymns to God, and the other prisoners were listening to them" (v. 25). As they sang, an earthquake rocked the prison, throwing open the doors. When the warden rushed in, Paul led him and his family to Christ. The jailer took them to a fountain and washed their wounds, then Paul baptized him, presumably in the water now tinted with his own blood.

And so, despite Paul's incarceration, the church continued to grow at great cost. Had you or I attended a service, we would have seen Lydia and her household, the slave girl, the jailer and his family, and probably some released prisoners. And they would have been singing.

I've often tried to imagine the scene at midnight when the two prisoners in the innermost cell—immobilized, bleeding, traumatized, their raw wounds untreated—began singing. It probably took them hours to process their pain and their painful emotions. But by midnight, they were ready to shift their attention from their wounds to their worship.

The lyrics were undoubtedly from the book of Psalms, and I've read through the Psalms trying to figure out the ones they might have chosen. Psalm 18:6–7 says, "In my distress I called to the LORD; I cried to my God for help. From his temple he heard my voice; . . . The earth trembled and quaked, and the foundations of the mountains shook."

That's exactly what happened in Acts 16. Additionally, Psalm 68:6 says: "He leads out the prisoners with singing."

It's pretty easy, then, to imagine that Paul and Silas had the words—the lyrics of psalms, hymns, and spiritual songs—already in their minds. They didn't have a hymnbook with them, and there were no words projected on the prison walls. They sang from memory. They had an internalized hymnbook in their heads. This came from their Jewish worship practices. Every practicing Jew knew many of the psalms by heart. They sang them in the synagogues, at the temple, as they traveled to their festivals, and in their private devotions.

We can learn from that. Apart from memorized scripture, there's nothing more crucial to our emotional and spiritual well-being than having a selection of memorized songs piping through our thoughts as needed.

Colossians 3:16 says: "Let the word of Christ dwell in you richly in all wisdom, teaching and admonishing one another in psalms and hymns and spiritual songs, singing with grace in your hearts to the Lord" (NKJV).

When the word of Christ fills your mind, it's natural for the songs of Christ to fill your heart.

A good hymn or praise song is a miniature Bible study, versified and set to music. Look at the book of Psalms. David, who was both a theologian and a musician, studied the Torah—the first five books of Moses. From his meditations, he created little Bible studies, versified with parallelism and set to music. He applied scripture to life and turned it into songs. That became the book of Psalms, and the Hebrew people memorized most or all of them.

From this heritage, Paul and Silas had a treasure trove of devotional material in their minds and hearts, and at the midnight hour it spilled out in singing. Paul was a Hebraic Jew and Silas was a Hellenistic Jew, but they both

WHEN THE WORD OF CHRIST FILLS YOUR MIND, IT'S NATURAL FOR THE SONGS OF CHRIST TO FILL YOUR HEART.

knew how to sing in the night, and they already had the songs in their minds and hearts.

In his gripping book, *Imprisoned with ISIS,* Petr Jasek describes being arrested in Sudan while working with persecuted Christians. He spent 445 days in brutal prisons. During this time, he recalled all the Scripture and all the hymns he knew.

On one occasion, a friend was able to get a hymnbook to him, but the prosecutor immediately took it away. Later the man summoned Petr and held up the hymnbook, asking, "What is this?"

"It's a collection of songs."

"Can you sing?"

"Of course I can," Petr said.

The prosecutor ordered, "Then sing me a song."

Petr decided to make the most of this opportunity, so he sang the wonderful hymn, "Thine Be the Glory." He sang all three verses, then said, "Let me tell you what this song is all about." And he shared Christ with his Muslim captor.[2]

I'm a product of the Jesus Revolution that swept America in the 1960s and '70s. Out of that revival came a new contemporary form of Christian music, which I championed and still do. I love good, solid, biblical, new music. Every generation needs to write its own songs. But I've also continued to champion the hymns. After all, the editors of the Psalms had songs dating from the time of Moses (Psalm 90) to post-exilic times (Psalm 137), a span of a thousand years. This shows us we need songs old and new. When Paul spoke of "psalms, hymns, and spiritual songs," he was clearly indicating a variety of styles and genres.

The problem facing pastors and worship leaders today is the short life span of modern Christian music. A recent study found that the average life of a popular modern worship song is three years, but that's generous.[3] A new song makes it to Christian radio, we sing it a few months, then it's gone. Most don't stay long enough to become a lifelong song of worship. That's why we need hymns alongside our worship songs. Otherwise we're depriving worshippers of the very thing Paul and Silas possessed—an internalized hymnbook in their minds.

While I love and sing the newer music, I cannot tell you how grateful I am for the classic hymns that have towered above the ages and outlived the trends and pop charts. Were I ever in a similar situation to what Paul and Silas experienced, I believe I would sing the songs I know the best and love the most. Those would include "O Worship the King," "Praise to the Lord, the Almighty," "Rejoice the Lord Is King," "Great Is Thy Faithfulness," and "Blessed Assurance."

These are the songs I sing to my great-grandkids. These are the songs that circulate through my mind when I'm pressed into the window seat of a plane, too tired to read. These are the songs that greet me when I awake in the morning and calm me when I go to bed at night.

Our spiritual well-being needs a set of songs we sing repeatedly over the course of our lifetime. Knowing the lyrics and loving the tunes will impact the memory and enrich the soul with all its attitudes, emotions, reactions, and needs.

How, then, can we develop our own mental collection of psalms, hymns, and spiritual songs?

First, use an online music service to create your own playlist and add some great hymns to it. My list has some newer classics on it along with many of my favorite hymns. I play it each morning as I shower and dress for the day, and it prepares me for my morning quiet time. At my writing desk, I have an instrumental list of songs. Even as I'm writing this, the music to "Joyful, Joyful, We Adore Thee" is playing quietly in the background.

Second, keep a hymnbook by your Bible. You can find hymnbooks at any used bookstore or online. Some newer ones are out now too. (My series of books, *Then Sings My Soul,* contains the words and music scores of many great hymns, along with the stories behind them.)

Third, let's ask our worship leaders to weave more hymns into the fabric of public worship services. Without damaging relationships, I believe we should really insist on a blending of the old and new in our worship—which, as I said, is in keeping with the makeup of the book of Psalms.

Fourth, learn to meditate on the hymns. Let them serve as a soundtrack for your mind.

Finally, pass on the hymns to your children and to the children in your church. It's the hymns we learn in childhood that engrave the deepest routes through our souls as we sing them over the course of our lives. Play them as your kids get ready for school or as you travel to ball practice. In days to come, our youngsters will badly need a soundtrack of holy songs streaming through their souls.

MEDITATE ON THE HYMNS. LET THEM SERVE AS A SOUNDTRACK FOR YOUR MIND.

My friend Bill Welte, director of America's Keswick, a multigenerational cross-cultural ministry in New Jersey, is an accomplished pianist. He told me about an older friend of his who was suffering from dementia. For many years this man had been a church music leader, but now he often became combative with his family. Most days he didn't know who they were.

One day they took him to the empty conference center and pushed his wheelchair to the front. Sitting at a piano, Bill started playing some classic hymns. Immediately the elderly man got up, walked up to the platform, and started leading an invisible congregation in singing. Bill said, "I must have played for thirty minutes, and he led the entire time without a hymnal. He didn't miss a word. He was filled with intense joy."

As soon as the man sat down again, his memory returned to its debilitated state. It was the great hymns, deeply embedded in his memory, that still created a melody in his soul.[4]

Just before my wife, Katrina, went to heaven, she became addled and frustrated. Her mind grew confused. As I lifted her into her wheelchair, I heard her muttering something, and I realized she was quoting a stanza from Charles Wesley's "O for a Thousand Tongues to Sing."

> *My gracious Master and my God,*
> *assist me to proclaim,*
> *to spread thro' all the earth abroad*
> *the honors of thy name.*[5]

She'd known that hymn from childhood, and as the Holy Spirit brought it to her mind, she quoted and repeated it. What a blessing for her and what a memory for me. She sang that song when she was a child. She sang it as a teenager. She sang it as a young adult. She sang it in all the churches we pastored. And she sang it in her final days. It was a set of lifelong lyrics that the fleeting music of today can never match.

Cliff Barrows, who directed the music for the Billy Graham meetings, once told me, "Rob, the great hymns of the faith flood through my thoughts day and night. It's a devotional exercise to endeavor to recall their words and stanzas."

Through song and suffering, the church was planted in Philippi, and through song and suffering, we, too, serve the Lord faithfully with joy, even in our midnight hours.

It takes awhile to move from pain to praise. This very morning I found myself in mental pain, and I reached for my trusty old hymnal and was helped. So whatever happens, build your own mental hymnbook. Begin today. Sing to the Lord a new song, but don't forget the old ones.

SING TO THE LORD A NEW SONG, BUT DON'T FORGET THE OLD ONES.

Whatever happens, keep a melody of praise in your heart.

Chapter 3

WHATEVER HAPPENS . . .

LAYER YOUR LIFE WITH GENEROSITY

(PHILIPPIANS 1:1)

Warner Davis grew up in the Democratic Republic of Congo where his parents were Methodist missionaries. He came to the United States to enroll at Asbury University, and he recently wrote about the experience in *Guideposts* magazine. It was in 1968. College back then wasn't as expensive as it is now, but the economy was much different. Warner needed $200 to cover his tuition. He skipped spring break to go door-to-door selling cookware, but with miserable results.

One morning he blurted out, "Lord, if you bless me financially this week, I promise I'll give 10 percent of my income to the church." By Saturday, he'd made $250. But he forgot his promise to the Lord.

Warner was serving as student pastor of a small church, and on Sunday he got up for his daily devotions. His reading that day took him to Malachi 3:6–12, where the Lord scolded the Israelites for not giving back to Him a portion of what He had given them. The Lord said, "Will a man rob God? Yet you have robbed Me!" (v. 8 NKJV). Warner quickly sat down and wrote a check for $10. Then he tore it up and wrote another for $15. Then he tore that one up, took a deep breath, and wrote one for $25. Going to church, he dropped the check into the collection plate.

On that Sunday two visitors—an elderly couple—showed up, which was unusual. As they left, they handed Warner an envelope. Inside was a personal gift for $25. Warner later found the address of the couple and visited them. "Why me?" he asked. "And why that Sunday? How did you know who I was?" The couple explained they had long followed his father's missionary work, and they felt an impulse to show their appreciation by giving something to his son. That Sunday seemed as good a day as any.

That lesson stayed with Warner Davis all his life. Never again, he said, did he have to try three times to write a check to the Lord before he got it right.[1]

The Philippians would have liked that story. Theirs was a leading city in Macedonia. Nearby were the towns of Thessalonica and Berea. The churches Paul planted in those cities have gone down in history for their generosity.

In Philippi, Lydia was a businesswoman dealing with a very expensive commodity—purple cloth, which was colored from a dye harvested from creatures of the sea. It was a high-end product, which meant Lydia was undoubtedly wealthy. As soon as she was converted, she opened her home to the missionary party—Paul, Silas, Timothy, and Luke. It must have been a large home, probably with servants, mosaics, patios, and spacious rooms. She would have told them, "It's yours to use." Her home became the meeting place for the church.

The next person converted was on the opposite end of the social spectrum—a slave girl, whose conversion led to the arrest and flogging of Paul and Silas. As we've seen, the missionaries' midnight singing led to the conversion of the jailer and his family. Acts 16:40 says, "After Paul and Silas came out of the prison, they went to Lydia's house, where they met with the brothers and sisters and encouraged them. Then they left." The authorities expelled them from the city—all except for Luke.

Notice the word "they." Luke, who had joined the party in Troas and introduced the "we" sections of the narrative, stayed behind in Philippi, where, as I said earlier, he may have been a student or professor at the medical school. His presence gave stability to the new congregation, and he undoubtedly encouraged the churches in Thessalonica and Berea as well.

These three churches—especially the Philippian—have gone down in history as the most generous, missionary-supporting congregations of the New Testament. Perhaps Lydia set the pace. Two entire chapters of 2 Corinthians are devoted to this. Look at verses 8:1–5:

> And now, brothers and sisters, we want you to know about the grace that God
> has given the Macedonian churches. In the midst of a very severe trial, their
> overflowing joy and their extreme poverty welled up in rich generosity. For I
> testify that they gave as much as they were able, and even beyond their ability.
> Entirely on their own, they urgently pleaded with us for the privilege of sharing
> in this service to the Lord's people. And they exceeded our expectations: They
> gave themselves first of all to the Lord, and then by the will of God also to us.

On this occasion, Paul was collecting benevolence funds for the poverty-stricken churches of Judea. The Macedonian churches understood the concept of giving to the Lord better than anyone else. God had given them the grace of giving.

The apostle Paul collected this offering and took it to Jerusalem in Acts 21. But his presence at the temple sparked another riot. He was arrested and sent to prison in Caesarea, where he spent two years. He finally appealed his case to the emperor and was sent to Rome, where he lived under house arrest for two years until the time came for him to stand trial. That's where the book of Acts ends in chapter 28.

The Philippians were following the news of all this. Apparently near the end of the two years, Paul was moved to a more secure location for his trial. When the Philippians heard this, they were alarmed.

"What can we do?" they asked. "How can we help him?"

They took up yet another offering. One of the church members—Epaphroditus—offered to take the offering to him and stay through the trial, helping and caring for Paul. After prayers and goodbyes, Epaphroditus left Philippi for the trip to Rome.

Matthew Harmon, who has studied the distance, estimates that the trip would have been between seven hundred and twelve hundred miles, depending on the route taken. The time of year would have determined whether sea travel was possible. Dr. Harmon wrote, "In the best conditions such a trip could be made by foot in about six weeks. In less favorable circumstances, it could take three months."[2]

Once in Rome, Epaphroditus tracked Paul down, gave him the money, and stayed with him. Unfortunately, Epaphroditus then became deathly ill, and instead of taking care of Paul, Paul had to take care of him. When Epaphroditus recovered well enough to travel, Paul sent him back to Philippi with a letter of friendship and gratitude. This is our letter to the Philippians. It's essentially a thank-you letter from Paul to his primary supporting church.

What can we learn from this?

Watch What God Is Doing Around the World

Stay attuned to the expansion of the kingdom of Christ around the world. In all of the New Testament, the church in Philippi was the prime example of a congregation that tracked and supported Paul's groundbreaking ministry. Their example has impacted the generosity of the church through the ages, and that, in turn, has impacted the world economy in greater ways than we know.

In 2008, the *Wall Street Journal* published an article about a Chinese economist named Zhao Xiao.[3] (Americanized, his name is Dr. Peter Zhao, pronounced *Zow*.) Zhao was a rising star in the Communist Party and an atheist. In the early 2000s, Chinese authorities asked him to lead an academic study to determine why America had the strongest economy. They wanted to figure out the secret of America's success and leverage it. But when Dr. Zhao brought back his report, the authorities didn't know what to do with it.

Dr. Zhao had one basic conclusion. America was founded on Judeo-Christian principles, and that biblical basis provided a tireless work ethic, a sense of honesty, a suppression of corruption, a motivation for excellence, a creative spirit, and a deep belief in generosity. He said that while China had rice shops on every corner, America had churches on every corner.

"The strong US economy is just on the surface. The backbone is the moral foundation,"[4] he said. Dr. Zhao wrote over two hundred articles about this.

Chuck Bentley, head of Crown Financial Ministries, read the *Wall Street Journal* article and instantly felt a deep burden to pray for this Chinese economist whom he'd never met.

Two years later, Chuck was at a financial conference in Orlando. Next to him was a table with ten Chinese men listening with headphones to the translation. Upon inquiry, he learned one of those men was the very one for whom he had been praying. He felt chills run over him as he met the Chinese economist. Chuck also learned that Dr. Zhao had become a follower of Jesus Christ. In writing about this, Bentley said:

> Churches that teach God's Word have an incalculable but profoundly positive impact on individuals and thus a nation's economy.
>
> Two things that provide a snapshot of the health and future of a nation: the number of healthy Bible believing churches and the number of entrepreneurs that are free to pursue their dream. Dr. Zhao was right; China needs God. But not just China; every pastor needs to understand they are creating "good economic actors" with the values, the character, and creative spirit that builds a personal economy and, in turn, contributes to the collective economic health of a nation.
>
> I have traveled to much of the world sharing this simple message. I have had the honor of teaching many times inside of China with my beloved friend Dr. Zhao. Neither of us plan to stop.[5]

Ask God to Give You the Grace of Giving

Our desire to support the cause of Christ is the outworking of God's grace in our lives. Second Corinthians 8:1 says, "And now, brothers and sisters, we want you to know about the grace that God has given the Macedonian churches."

OUR DESIRE TO SUPPORT THE CAUSE OF CHRIST IS THE OUTWORKING OF GOD'S GRACE IN OUR LIVES.

I've found—and this is after seventy years of working on it—that whenever I receive a paycheck of some sort, my first and most excited thought is how I can use a portion of it to support the Lord's work. I love having that feeling, but it's simply grace. Ask God to give you the grace of giving. Seriously. Start praying that right now.

Give as God Leads You, Despite the Circumstances

Look at 2 Corinthians 8:2 again: "In the midst of a very severe trial, their overflowing joy and their extreme poverty welled up in rich generosity." The key words here are "welled up." Think of a spring in which the water rises to the surface by itself and wells up to overflowing.

What's beneath the surface? What forces are pushing the water of financial support to the top of our agenda and overflowing with what verse 2 calls "rich generosity"?

Three things: a severe trial, overflowing joy, and extreme poverty.

Apparently, some kind of opposition or persecution had befallen the churches in Macedonia, and it made them realize their temporary possessions were not as important as their eternal riches. In the middle of their trials, God gave them joy, and even though they were facing extreme poverty, the Lord provided something special for them to give. And it all welled up into rich generosity.

There are always ways to be generous despite your circumstances.

Offer the Totality of Your Life to the Lord

Don't just offer what you have—offer all that you are to the Lord. Make a full surrender to Him. That's what Paul said the church at Philippi did.

Look at 2 Corinthians 8:3–5: "For I testify that they gave as much as they were able, and even beyond their ability. Entirely on their own, they urgently pleaded with us for the privilege of sharing in this service to the Lord's people. And they exceeded our expectations: They gave themselves first of all to the Lord, and then by the will of God also to us."

To recap: Paul, Silas, Timothy, and Luke entered Philippi in AD 49, established the church, and departed, leaving Luke behind. The Christians at Philippi and the neighboring towns followed Paul's ministry and faithfully sent him gifts. In about AD 62, the Philippians sent him another gift by the hand of Epaphroditus, who intended to stay with Paul through his legal trial in Rome, but he became deathly sick. Paul tended to him, helped him recover, and sent him back with great appreciation. Epaphroditus returned home, bearing the letter to the Philippians with him.

It was the overflowing generosity of the Macedonian churches that occasioned the book of Philippians.

Don't you find it exciting to be part of a global movement that's changing the world and hastening the day of Christ? The whole world is ours to reach. We never know how God will use whatever we render into His hands. So whatever happens, add generosity to your virtues.

Chapter 4

WHATEVER HAPPENS . . .

RELY ON REVITALIZING GRACE

(PHILIPPIANS 1:1-2)

Mr. Christian, the hero in John Bunyan's *Pilgrim's Progress*, had just started out for the Celestial City when he stopped at Interpreter's house and learned helpful lessons for his journey. Interpreter took him from room to room displaying various items of significance. In one room a fireplace blazed with a roaring fire, but the devil was throwing buckets of water on the flames to douse them.

Christian asked in amazement, "How does the fire keep burning?"

Interpreter beckoned him through the door to the backside of the wall where a man behind the heath was pouring a constant stream of oil onto the flame, making it unquenchable.

How grateful we are for the secret supply of grace and peace that floods our hearts by the Holy Spirit. The book of Philippians begins on this note:

"Paul and Timothy, servants of Christ Jesus, to all God's holy people in Christ Jesus at Philippi, together with the overseers and deacons. Grace and peace to you from God our Father and the Lord Jesus Christ" (Philippians 1:1–2).

There's enough truth in those two verses to fill an ocean, but for the sake of simplicity let me show you three grammatical prepositions that link the clauses and allow us to follow the logic of Paul's words. Prepositions are just little things, some of our smallest words, but they're very important. In a parade, it makes a big difference if you're *before* the elephant or *behind* the elephant. At a funeral, it's important whether you're *above* the ground or *below* it.

So let's look at Paul's three primary prepositions. He tells us that he and Timothy are "servants *of* Christ Jesus," sent to all the people who are "*in* Christ Jesus." Then he extends to his readers grace and peace "*from* God our Father."

Paul listed those in the order that was natural in the writing of his letter, but let's tackle them in the order they unfold in our lives.

Saints in Christ

Paul addressed his letter to "all God's holy people in Christ Jesus at Philippi." Most translations say, "to all the saints in Philippi," but the New International Version uses the phrase "holy people" because *saints* has become a confusing term.

If you asked a person on the street or even at your church to name a saint for you, they might come up with Saint Francis of Assisi or maybe Mother Teresa. Maybe they'd say, "Well, my grandmother was a saint. She was the saintliest person I've ever known."

In the New Testament, however, the word *saint* simply indicated a Christ follower. The Greek term is *hagios*, often translated *holy, set apart, pure*. It was used among secular Greeks to describe something engendering awe. It also came to describe a temple or sanctuary containing beautiful and sacred things not accessible to the public.[1]

In the Old Testament, the equivalent Hebrew term described the God of Israel, His name, and the things connected to Him. We read about holy ground, the holy temple, the holy place, the holy of holies. God's Old Testament people were to be holy, keeping His laws and reflecting His purity to the nations of the earth.

In the New Testament, God the Father is described as holy and so is God the Son. God the Holy Spirit actually has the word in His title. But to our surprise, we also discover that we who know Christ as our Lord are called saints or, as the NIV says, "God's holy people."

It's important for us to think of ourselves in those terms. Our self-image and behavior are influenced by how we talk about ourselves to ourselves. If you think of yourself as worthless, unlovable, or inadequate, you'll begin to act that way. But if you say, "I am one of God's holy people, one of God's saints," that will also affect the way you live.

We're God's holy people in a twofold way. First, as followers of Christ, *instantaneous* holiness is conferred on us at the moment of belief. Second, as we grow in Christ, the Lord's *progressive* holiness develops within us. We can see both of these aspects in Hebrews 10.

Hebrews 10:10 says, "We have been made holy through the sacrifice of the body of Jesus Christ once for all." The moment we receive Christ as Savior, we are made righteous in God's sight. Our sins are transferred to Christ, and His holiness is transferred to us.

Let me say it again: If you think of yourself as worthless, unlovable, or inadequate, you'll begin to act that way. But if you say, "I am one of God's holy people, one of God's saints," that will also affect the way you live.

Consider Edward Creasy, a young man who joined the British army and fought in France and the Middle East during World War I. In May of 1921, he was captured and condemned to be shot by a Polish firing squad. But he told them: "The Union Jack [the flag of the British Empire], though invisible, is around me. You will hit the British flag if you fire. You dare not do it."

The firing squad hesitated, then lowered their weapons.[2]

In the same way, the righteousness of Jesus Christ is wrapped around us. We're shielded by His enveloping holiness. The devil may accuse us, but he cannot successfully attack and condemn us. We may not yet be all we should be, but we are wrapped in and vested with the holiness of Christ.

Four verses later, in Hebrews 10:14, we read: "For by one sacrifice he has made perfect forever those who are being made holy." Do you see the twofold aspect of this? You *have been made* holy (v. 10), and you *are being made* holy (v. 14).

David Allen, in his commentary on Hebrews, wrote, "The author is making good use of the Greek tense system here to contrast the perfect finished work of Christ on the cross and its sanctifying effect on believers (verse 10) with the ongoing work of progressive sanctification here in verse 14."[3]

Theologians use the phrase "already but not yet" to describe this process. We are instantaneously declared holy when we receive Christ as Savior, but we progressively become more holy as we follow Him in discipleship. We are God's holy people *in* Christ.

That was Paul's trademark phrase—*in Christ*.

> WE ARE INSTANTANEOUSLY DECLARED HOLY WHEN WE RECEIVE CHRIST AS SAVIOR, BUT WE PROGRESSIVELY BECOME MORE HOLY AS WE FOLLOW HIM IN DISCIPLESHIP.

The word "in" means to be positioned or placed within a certain environment. Think of the atmosphere. We're surrounded by air, and air is within us, in our lungs. If we're locked in a vacuum chamber and the air gives out, we're no longer in the air and the air is no longer in us. We'll die.

When we receive Jesus Christ as Savior, we are enveloped in Jesus. He is the environment of the soul. He is in us, and we are in Him—His holy people.

Servants of Christ

Philippians 1:1 also talks about being servants of Christ. The Greek word *doulos* literally means *slave*. Paul used this term fifty-nine times in his writings, but it has a double connotation.

First, it connotes humility. Vast portions of the Roman Empire were made up of professionals—lawyers, financial experts, clothiers, chefs, administrators, educators, and so on—but they were employed by whoever owned them. The apostle Paul attacked the institution of slavery in a powerful way in the book of Philemon, and he encouraged slaves, if possible, to seek their freedom.[4] Yet he also said we are all slaves of Jesus Christ.[5]

Further, Paul used this same term of Christ in chapter 2, telling us how

Jesus took upon Himself the very nature of a *doulos* (Philippians 2:7). Our Lord was never owned by anyone, yet He became a servant, a slave, to all.

One of the most noted devotional writers of the last two hundred years was Andrew Murray of South Africa. Many of his books are based on his sermons, but for two years he literally lost his voice. He suffered from a mysterious condition that rendered him virtually speechless. He had to take a sabbatical from the pulpit. During this time, he studied the subject of humility and learned the lessons by experiencing them. He later published a fabulous book on the subject of humility, in which he said:

> There is nothing so divine and heavenly as being the servant and helper of all. The faithful servant, who recognizes his position, finds a real pleasure in supplying the wants of the master or his guests. When we see that humility is something infinitely deeper than contrition and accept it as our participation in the life of Jesus, we shall begin to learn that it is our true nobility, and that to prove it in being servants of all is the highest fulfillment of our destiny as [people] created in the image of God.[6]

That quote points out the paradox of being a slave. Biblical commentators have discussed this a great deal. On the one hand, the word *servant* connotes our humble position, but at the same time, to be identified in Scripture as a "servant of the Lord" was an exalted honor. Here are some examples:

- Psalm 105:26 says "[The Lord] sent Moses his servant, and Aaron, whom he had chosen."
- Joshua 24:29 calls Joshua the "son of Nun, the servant of the Lord."
- Ezekiel 34:23 identifies David as "my servant."
- Daniel 9:6 admits that the people had not "listened to your servants the prophets, who spoke in your name."

This is one of the great paradoxes and deepest mysteries of the Christian experience. To be the Lord's servant is to simultaneously be humbled and honored—and according to Philippians 1:1, *we* are both saints in Christ Jesus and servants of Christ Jesus.

Supplied from Christ

In Christ, as a believer, you are supplied with abundant grace and are the heir of every single blessing God has ever invented. *Grace* is a five-letter word made up of a billion blessings. Because God is infinite, we have never-ceasing grace.

Read these five fabulous verses aloud:

- "Praise be to the God and Father of our Lord Jesus Christ, who has blessed us . . . with every spiritual blessing in Christ." (Ephesians 1:3)
- "God is able to bless you abundantly, so that in all things at all times, having all that you need, you will abound in every good work." (2 Corinthians 9:8)
- "Every good and perfect gift is from above, coming down from the Father of the heavenly lights." (James 1:17)
- "Blessed be the Lord, who daily loads us with benefits." (Psalm 68:19 NKJV)
- "From his abundance we have all received one gracious blessing after another." (John 1:16 NLT)

Because of God's abundant blessings, we're also flooded with peace. We have peace with God and the peace of God, which we'll get to later in Philippians 4. The devil can neither rob us of our blessings nor permanently disrupt our peace, however much he tries.

I know this from experience, don't you? None of us have easy lives, and mine hasn't always been easy. There were times I was so desolate I didn't think I could be reassembled. But thus far I've never had an experience, however hard, in which I didn't find what I needed in the words of Scripture, the stanzas of hymns, and the closet of prayer. Even recently when I was very low, as I sat at my desk with my open Bible, I almost physically felt the moment the Lord poured oil onto the fire and strength into my soul. Can you relate? I suspect you can. And one thing I know—you can always rely on God's revitalizing grace. We are saints in Christ, servants of Christ, and supplied by Christ with all we need.

Annie J. Flint, a disabled hymnist who knew about this from firsthand experience, wrote:

IN CHRIST, AS A BELIEVER, YOU ARE SUPPLIED WITH ABUNDANT GRACE AND ARE THE HEIR OF EVERY SINGLE BLESSING GOD HAS EVER INVENTED.

His love has no limit, His grace has no measure,
His power no boundary known unto men,
For out of His infinite riches in Jesus
He giveth and giveth and giveth again.[7]

Chapter 5

WHATEVER HAPPENS . . .

REMEMBER GOD IS STILL WORKING ON YOU

(PHILIPPIANS 1:3-8)

I try to keep a healthy perspective, don't you? As of now, I've not faced a major, sudden, traumatic tragedy in my life, for which I'm grateful. But I've had a hard series of recent losses, and I've adjusted more slowly than expected. I stepped away from my life's work as a senior pastor to care for my wife until she passed away. After that, I tried to continue serving my church of four decades, but that became untenable, so I quietly slipped out the back door. Then one of my dearest friends died prematurely. And now, to make matters worse, I haven't been able to shake prolonged COVID fatigue.

One morning while trying to rally my spirits, I decided to study the Old Testament book of Ezra and I found this verse: "So this Sheshbazzar came and laid the foundations of the house of God in Jerusalem. From that day to the present it has been under construction but is not yet finished" (Ezra 5:16). In capital letters, I wrote in the margin: "THAT'S ME!" I'm still under construction, but not yet finished.

It's with this same emphasis that Paul opened his letter to the Philippians:

I thank my God every time I remember you. In all my prayers for all of you, I always pray with joy because of your partnership in the gospel from the first day until now, being confident of this, that he who began a good work in you will carry it on to completion until the day of Christ Jesus. (Philippians 1:3–6)

This is Paul's opening prayer for the church in Philippi—and for us. It's actually one long sentence in the Greek and continues through verse 8. As he sometimes did, Paul became so excited he didn't stop for punctuation or pauses. The New International Version turns Philippians 1:3–8 into four sentences and two brief paragraphs to simplify it for us.

Thankfulness

Paul began by saying, "I thank my God every time I remember you" (v. 3). He could have said, "I thank God," but he said, "I thank *my* God." He was practicing the presence of God. He thought of God as very personal, very near.

Several years ago I read about a missionary—I think it was Amy Carmichael—who kept a thanksgiving list alongside her prayer list. Every day she jotted down something for which she was thankful. I decided to do the same, and every morning I added something new to the list. It might be something as simple as a hot shower or as significant as a good lab result from the doctor.

But in studying Philippians 1:3, I became convicted. I tend to thank God for *things*. Paul thanked God for *people*. You can follow that theme through his letters. There's no doubt he was grateful for all his blessings, but most of his expressions of thanksgiving involved individuals. Since considering this verse, I've taken more time to list two items each day for which I'm thankful: a *what* and a *who*.

I TEND TO THANK GOD FOR *THINGS*. PAUL THANKED GOD FOR *PEOPLE*.

Methodist evangelist William Stidger preached in tents across the nation and wrote a newspaper column. One day he sat around a table with people who were complaining about everything. He left the table, determined to become a grateful person and to thank God for both things and people. The first person who flashed into his mind was an English teacher who had instilled in him a love of literature and poetry. He felt she had done a lot to prepare him for his later ministry.

That evening, he wrote to her, thanking her for her contribution to his life. A few days later he received this letter in return, and she addressed him using his childhood name:

> My Willie, I can't tell you how much your note meant to me. I am in my eighties, living alone in a small room, cooking my own meals, lonely, like the last leaf of autumn that lingers behind. You'll be interested to know that I taught in school for more than fifty years, and yours is the first note of appreciation I have ever received. It came on a blue, cold morning, and it cheered me as nothing has done in many years.[1]

This kind of gratitude doesn't come naturally. It takes training. It takes practice. We have to work at it all the time.

If you want to truly change your personality, search for how many times the Bible uses the terms *thank, thanks, thanksgiving, gratitude,* and *grateful*. Make a serious study of this. Write down the verses, study the context, track down the cross-references, systematize them, and choose some of them to memorize.

The British poet George Herbert prayed, "Thou hast given so much to me, give me one more thing—a grateful heart."[2]

GRATITUDE DOESN'T COME NATURALLY. IT TAKES TRAINING. IT TAKES PRACTICE. WE HAVE TO WORK AT IT ALL THE TIME.

Prayerfulness

Alongside thankfulness comes prayerfulness. Paul said, "In all my prayers for all of you." Then, in verse 19, we read: "I know that through your prayers and

God's provision of the Spirit of Jesus Christ what has happened to me will turn out for my deliverance."

The prayers were flying in both directions.

Just after World War II, as the world was still processing what had happened, missionary Frank Laubach wrote an urgent book about prayer that swept across the nation and impacted millions of people. He called on every believer to unite in intercession for one another and for our leaders. He gave several examples of how we can learn to pray with greater frequency for others:

- He suggested that when reading about a world leader in the news, we pause for ten seconds to pray for that person.
- He encouraged people in churches to keep their eyes open while the preacher was giving the sermon, but to be praying for him silently as he expounded the Scripture.
- He trained himself to throw a cloak of prayer around those he met during the day. He prayed silently for people as they approached him and for those he traveled with.
- He told of one man who wrote out a prayer every evening, offered it to God, and then threw it in the fireplace, watching the smoke as it burned and ascended into heaven like the incense of the Old Testament.
- He described another man who had a clock that struck on the quarter hour. The man kept a set of prayer cards with ministries he supported. Every time the clock chimed, he offered a brief prayer for the ministry on the top card, then put it on the bottom of the pack so that he was circulating through his prayer concerns every quarter hour.

Laubach used these examples to urge people to find ways of praying without ceasing. He said, "Enough people praying enough will release into the human bloodstream the mightiest medicine in the universe, for we shall be the channels through whom God can exert His infinite power."[3]

Paul wrote with similar passion, saying, in effect, "I am praying for you every time I think about you. I am praying and counting my blessings, and as you pray for me, too, I know I'll receive God's provision of the Spirit and what has happened will turn out for good."

Through prayer, we release into our bloodstreams the mightiest medicine known to exist in this universe.

Cheerfulness

Paul also prayed cheerfully: "In all my prayers for all of you, I always pray with joy" (v. 4). This is the first of sixteen times Paul used the word *joy* in this letter. Oh, how many times during periods of discouragement have I read through Philippians, circling every reference to joy and rejoicing.

Paul was thankful for the Philippians' partnership, or *koinonia*. This partnership started with his original visit to Philippi in Acts 16. It continued through frequent correspondence and included their joint endeavors in sharing the gospel. It summed up the long-term friendship they had enjoyed over the years.

Paul prayed with joy because He knew God was working in the Philippian believers, and that brings us to a favorite verse—Philippians 1:6. "Being confident of this," Paul said, "that he who began a good work in you will carry it on to completion until the day of Christ Jesus."

Some commentators think this was a reference only to the financial partnership extended to him by the Philippians—their fellowship in helping finance his work. He was certain God would lead them to continue that. But that seems to be a narrow interpretation. I believe this verse means just what we feel it should mean—God started doing something in Philippi in Acts 16. He started doing something in Lydia, in the servant girl, in the prisoners, in the jailer, and in the whole church.

And that work will continue until we stand before Christ in the perfection of eternity.

A bit later, the apostle wrote, "It is God who works in you to will and to act in order to fulfill his good purpose" (Philippians 2:13).

I remember a college classmate who sat down with me and drew a little chart. It had three columns.

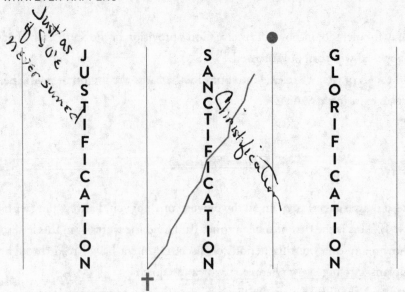

Pointing to the first column, he said, "This one is justification. That's what happened to you when you received Christ as Savior. That's your past—when God saved you from the penalty of your sins." Then he pointed to the other side of the chart.

"On the other side is glorification. That's what will happen in the future when you're raptured or resurrected. God will save you from the very presence of sin. In between," he continued, "is sanctification. That's the process that happens to you now as you grow in Christ and are continually saved from the power of sin. It might go up and down a bit, but it will end with glory. When you put all three together, you have salvation in its totality. You *were* saved, *are being* saved, and *will be* saved."

All three aspects of my friend's chart are found in Philippians 1:6 and are usually summed up in three words: *justification* (He who began a good work in you); *sanctification* (will carry it on); and *glorification* (to completion when Christ comes again).

I've never forgotten that chart, but recently I've made a change to it. Instead of the word *sanctification*, I've started using the word *Christification*. We are becoming more and more like Him.

Ray Ortlund wrote a column for the *Gospel Coalition* in which he recalled his father giving him a Bible for his seventeenth birthday. On the first page, his dad wrote: "Bud, nothing could be greater than to have a son—a son who loves the Lord and walks with Him. Your mother and I have found this book our dearest treasure. Be a student of the Bible, and your life will be full of blessing. We love you. Dad." And beneath the word "Dad" was the Scripture reference Philippians 1:6.

The first thing Ray did was open to Philippians 1:6.

In his column, Ray said: "Apart from the words my dad spoke to me the day he led me to Christ, what he wrote above was his greatest statement to me ever. It has always proven true. I can hardly read it today without weeping."[4]

In the words of a little song we used to sing, "He's still working on me, to make me what I need to be."[5] It's taking longer than it should, but He is patient. We have to remember that. I don't know about you, but the one person in this world with whom I have the most trouble is Mr. M. E. Dude.

M. E. has a temper. He says stupid things. He lets irritations get to him. He wants to do things he shouldn't, see things he shouldn't, think things he shouldn't. M. E. requires a lot of spiritual maintenance. This character can absolutely drive me crazy.

But by God's grace, if I have anything to do with it (and I do), Mr. M. E. Dude is going to become more like H. I. M.

> *The work Thou hast in me begun,*
> *Will by Thy grace be fully done.*[6]

Chapter 6

WHATEVER HAPPENS . . .

INVIGORATE YOUR LIFE THROUGH PRAYER

(PHILIPPIANS 1:9-11)

The psalmist prayed, "Invigorate my soul so I can praise you well" (Psalm 119:175 MSG). The word *invigorate* means "to put vigor into, to fill with energy." Sometimes we think of prayer as a fatiguing chore, when, in truth, it should be invigorating fellowship with the One who can fill us with energy so we can praise Him better.

One of the simplest ways to invigorate yourself or someone else through prayer is by learning the words Paul composed as his prayer for the Philippians. It's one of the most powerful in Scripture.

> This is my prayer: that your love may abound more and more in knowledge and depth of insight, so that you may be able to discern what is best and may be pure and blameless for the day of Christ, filled with the fruit of righteousness that comes through Jesus Christ—to the glory and praise of God. (Philippians 1:9–11)

41

In this passage in Philippians, Paul explained the virtuous cycle of Christification—how God carries on to completion the good work He has begun in us (v. 6). There are six steps to the process, and Paul prayed them into the Philippian church. Were you to learn and apply this prayer rigorously yourself, it would energize your personality.

Treat Others Lovingly

During the years between the Old Testament and the New Testament, a group of Jewish scholars in Egypt translated the Hebrew Bible—our Old Testament—into Greek. This became known as the Septuagint. Paul read and studied the Septuagint alongside his Hebrew Bible, and he started his prayer for the Philippian church by asking God that their "love may abound more and more."

The Septuagint used several Greek words to translate *love*, including the previously obscure word *agape*. The translators infused this term with fresh meaning to describe the sweet and superlative love of Almighty God.

New Testament writers then seized on this word, making *agape* an exclusively wondrous term. It is God's own true love, supercharged with grace, that can be channeled through us by God's Spirit. This kind of love doesn't ask what this person can do for me. It asks instead what *I can do* for this person.

Many of us have followed Tim Tebow because of his outspoken witness for Christ and the ups and downs of his athletic career. In a recent interview, he said, "The same year I was voted one of the most popular athletes in America, I was cut from my team. So in the same year, am I going to be at the high, or am I going to be at the low? I'm so grateful that when I hold on to God's truth, I don't have to be either—I am who God says I am."

Then he said:

The first verse my parents made me memorize as a five-year-old boy was "The greatest among you will be a servant. Whoever exalts himself will be humbled, but whoever humbles himself will be exalted." I didn't understand it, but my parents knew I was so competitive, and I wanted to play and I loved it. And so before we would play, we had to memorize Scripture verses, and for me, they were primarily on humility. . . . Sometimes it feels like you're on a roller coaster, but we get to get off and hold on to a firm foundation—and that's the Word of God.[1]

We jump onto the virtuous cycle when we realize that one day we may be the most popular person around and the next day we may be cut from the team, but it's all right because we are who God says we are—and our lives are intended to be marked by humility, seeking to meet the needs of our husband, wife, children, fellow students or employees, or the strangers that cross our paths.

Make Decisions Wisely

As we grow in *agape*, we make wiser decisions because we develop greater knowledge and depth of insight. We see things more clearly. Verses 9 and 10 go on to ask that their love would "abound more and more *in knowledge and depth of insight, so that you may be able to discern what is best*" (emphasis mine).

> AS WE GROW IN *AGAPE*, WE MAKE WISER DECISIONS BECAUSE WE DEVELOP GREATER KNOWLEDGE AND DEPTH OF INSIGHT.

As we let God's "servanting" love increasingly control us, we learn more about His will and His ways. Every decision has consequences, and one bad decision can reap a whirlwind. I read about a girl known for her good grades and kindheartedness. She never got into trouble herself, but she chose to hang out with people who were not like that. They were partying, and one of the girls shot off a flare gun in the house. The house caught fire and three small children were killed. The girl and her three friends were sent to prison. In the courthouse, the girl said she'd "made a bad decision that turned into the worst mistake of my life."[2]

One bad decision leads to another, creating a downward cycle, the very opposite of what God wants for us. Through the years, I've made bad decisions too. But the more time I spend in Scripture—reading it, studying it, memorizing it, pondering it—the more I'm able to grow in knowledge and depth of insight so I can discern what is best. One of my frequent prayers comes from an old hymn:

> *Teach me thy way, O Lord; teach me thy way!*
> *Thy guiding grace afford; teach me thy way.*
> *Help me to walk aright, more by faith, less by sight.*
> *Lead me with heav'nly light; teach me thy way!*[3]

Renowned theologian J. I. Packer wrote about the process of going to the Lord concerning everything that comes up, that we might know what to do and how to react. He said:

"Going to Him" is an umbrella phrase that covers three things: praying; meditating, which includes thinking, reflecting, drawing conclusions from Scripture, and applying them directly to oneself in Jesus' presence; and holding oneself open throughout the process to specific illumination from the Holy Spirit. . . .

These Christians cope with events in a spirit of peace, joy, and eagerness to see what God will do next. Others, however, who are no less committed to Jesus as their Savior, never master this art of habitually going to him about life's challenges.[4]

IF WE GO TO GOD IN EVERYTHING, WE'LL HAVE WISDOM AND DISCERNMENT ON EVERY NEEDED OCCASION—WHICH IS JUST ABOUT ALWAYS.

If we go to God in everything, we'll have wisdom and discernment on every needed occasion—which is just about always.

Build Inward Purity

As we do that, it stands to reason we'll develop inward purity: "And this is my prayer: that your love may abound more and more in knowledge and depth of insight, so that you may be able to discern what is best *and may be pure and blameless for the day of Christ*" (emphasis mine).

Pure and *blameless* are words that point to personal holiness.

Cicero, a Roman thinker who died about a generation before Jesus was born, said, "If you have a garden and a library, you have everything you need."

I'm fortunate to have a library with a door to my garden. Whenever I'm writing or working on sermons, I'll work for a while, then go into the garden and water things and pull weeds. Sometimes I use a hoe, but there is something satisfying about grabbing a weed by the stem, pulling it out by the roots, shaking off the dirt, and tossing it away. Then I'll go back to my library and study awhile.

I do the same thing in my interior life. I continually go back and forth from my Bible to my behavior. I'll spend time in the sixty-six books of God's library, and then I'll work on watering the good habits in my life and weeding out the bad ones. I've been working on it for a long time, and the garden of my life isn't yet all I want it to be. But as long as I live, I'm going to work at eradicating weeds from my life and watering the plants that belong to faith and obedience.

What does that lead to? To serving God continually.

> AS LONG AS I LIVE, I'M GOING TO WORK AT ERADICATING WEEDS FROM MY LIFE AND WATERING THE PLANTS THAT BELONG TO FAITH AND OBEDIENCE.

Serve God Continually

Look at our verses again: "And this is my prayer: that your love may abound more and more in knowledge and depth of insight, so that you may be able to discern what is best and may be pure and blameless for the day of Christ, *filled with the fruit of righteousness*" (emphasis mine).

The word *fruit* is a metaphor, a symbol. What is the fruit of righteousness? What does it mean? Remember Paul was a student of the Hebrew Scriptures and the Greek Septuagint—our Old Testament. This is an Old Testament phrase. You can find it in Psalm 72:3; Amos 6:12; and Proverbs 11:30. It refers to the behavior of a righteous person.

This is the outward manifestation of our inward holiness. This is what others see when they observe our lives.

Embody Christ Daily

As the virtuous cycle continues, we find ourselves enjoying Christ more and more richly. Read this prayer once more. "And this is my prayer: that your love may abound more and more in knowledge and depth of insight, so that you may be able to discern what is best and may be pure and blameless for the day of Christ, filled with the fruit of righteousness that comes *through Jesus Christ*—to the glory and praise of God" (emphasis mine).

This is the greatest secret of the Christian experience. Katrina and I both learned this through the teaching of Major Ian Thomas, the British Bible expositor. He said:

> The Lord Jesus Christ claims the use of your body, your whole being, your complete personality, so that as you give yourself to Him through the eternal Spirit, He may give Himself to you through the eternal Spirit, that all your activity as a human being on earth may be His activity in and through you; that every step you take, every word you speak, everything you do, everything you are, may be an expression of the Son of God living in you.[5]

I often read the Major's books because he constantly reminds me that only Christ can live the Christian life, and He does it by the Holy Spirit, who makes us channels for Himself. When we're Spirit-filled, our thoughts, choices, reactions, responses, and decisions will reflect the mind of Christ. This is the growing Christ-life within us.

Glorify God Greatly

All of the above results in glory and praise to God. This is the virtuous cycle. It's not something that happens once. It cycles over and over in our lives until we circle all the way to heaven. We experience the *agape* of God, and it works on our hearts. That clarifies our thinking so we make better decisions. We build inward purity and begin serving God continually. We do that only when we embody Christ daily, and it leads to praise.

Like the psalmist said, "Invigorate my soul so I can praise you well" (Psalm 119:175 MSG).

> WE EXPERIENCE THE *AGAPE* OF GOD, AND IT WORKS ON OUR HEARTS. THAT CLARIFIES OUR THINKING SO WE MAKE BETTER DECISIONS.

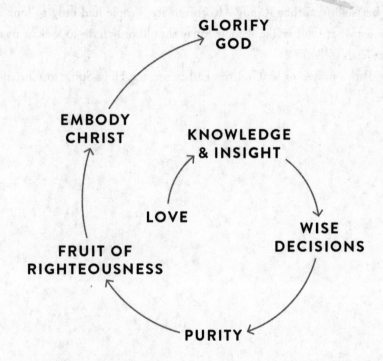

Say Paul's prayer to reinvigorate your life and use it to target someone else in prayer. Imagine bombarding an unsuspecting prodigal child with a prayer like this.

As a pastor, I'm always searching for ways to visualize Christlikeness. Here's a story I recently came across, and perhaps you'll relate to its ending. Most of us have seen Mt. Rushmore in pictures if we haven't visited it. A man named Gutzon Borglum first envisioned turning that mountain into the faces of four famous Americans. Borglum was fascinated with Lincoln, and he studied every hair on his head, every line on his face. He'd created multiple impressions of

Lincoln. Just before launching his project on Mt. Rushmore, Borglum took a ten-ton block of marble and chipped and carved and fashioned it into the head of Abraham Lincoln. When Lincoln's son Robert saw the work, he exclaimed, "I never expected to see my father again."[6]

The people of this world never again expect to see the likes of Jesus of Nazareth, but God is active and busy, chipping and carving and fashioning each one of us into the likeness of Jesus Christ.

As bestselling author Randy Alcorn put it, "People had only to look at Jesus to see what God is like. People today should only have to look at us to see what Jesus is like."[7]

Use Paul's prayer to let God the Father use the Holy Spirit to Christify your life.

Chapter 7

WHATEVER HAPPENS . . .

REPLACE GLOOMY THOUGHTS WITH GLORIOUS ONES

(PHILIPPIANS 1:12-18)

Last year during a speaking engagement in Tupelo, Mississippi, I checked out of my hotel and started my truck. It roared like a motorcycle with no muffler. During the night somebody had cut off and stolen my catalytic converter. This caused no end of problems. I had to leave my truck behind, rent a car, deal with insurance, and send somebody back to fetch my truck. After all that, the vehicle still wasn't working right, so I left it at the dealership while on another trip.

When I returned, I used a ride-sharing app to take me to the dealership for my truck. As I sat in the back seat, I noticed a Bible in the seat pocket. I asked the young man about it. He said it had belonged to his dear, departed aunt, and he liked to keep it close to remind him of her. I told him he should read it. I shared some verses I'd read that morning in my own Bible.

He listened with unusual interest, so I explained from Scripture how to have a relationship with God through Jesus Christ. By the time we got to the dealership, he wanted to pray, asking God for salvation—which he did.

*Looking
Yours & him*

That's when I understood why the Lord had allowed someone to steal my catalytic converter—it had set off a chain reaction that led to the young man's salvation.

WHAT IF YOU KNEW THAT EVERY GLOOMY THING WOULD LEAD TO GLORIOUS RESULTS UNDER THE GUIDING PROVIDENCE OF GOD?

Bad things happen all the time, but what if you knew that every gloomy thing would lead to glorious results under the guiding providence of God? That's what Paul next told the Philippians. They were distressed at all that had happened to him—the loss of his fourth missionary journey, his imprisonment in Caesarea, his shipwreck on Malta, and his looming trial in Rome. But Paul wasn't gloomy in the least. Here's what he told them:

> Now I want you to know, brothers and sisters, that what has happened to me has actually served to advance the gospel. As a result, it has become clear throughout the whole palace guard and to everyone else that I am in chains for Christ. And because of my chains, most of the brothers and sisters have become confident in the Lord and dare all the more to proclaim the gospel without fear.
>
> It is true that some preach Christ out of envy and rivalry, but others out of goodwill. The latter do so out of love, knowing that I am put here for the defense of the gospel. The former preach Christ out of selfish ambition, not sincerely, supposing that they can stir up trouble for me while I am in chains. But what does it matter? The important thing is that in every way, whether from false motives or true, Christ is preached. And because of this I rejoice. (Philippians 1:12–18)

This is the Philippian version of Romans 8:28, the verse that says, "And we know that all things work together for good to those who love God, to those who are the called according to *His* purpose" (NKJV). I wrote a book devoted to that subject entitled *God Works All Things Together for Your Good*. In the prologue, I said:

> Problems can last a long time, but they can't last forever. Promises can, and God's promises do. . . . We live in a world of catastrophes and calamities,

and none of us knows what will happen next. Without God's oversight, our futures are like scraps of paper scattering in the wind. But under His oversight, they're like pages of hope indelibly written by grace. The Scriptures teach we have a God who turns problems inside out—all our perils and perplexities. . . . In Christ, we have an ironclad, unfailing, all-encompassing, God-given guarantee that every single circumstance in life will sooner or later turn out well for those committed to Him.[1]

Paul had written Romans 8:28 three or four years before his imprisonment, but now he demonstrated it in his own circumstances. I want to base my outline on verse 12, where Paul wrote, "What has happened to me has actually served to advance the gospel."

What Has Happened

Years ago, there was a television series called *The West Wing*, and in one dramatic episode, an assassin fired at President Bartlet. He and several of his staff were wounded. The episode closed with Bartlet looking through the windows of the hospital intensive care unit. Still stunned, he said simply, "Look what happened." It was such a simple sentence, but it expressed the shock we feel when unexpected things take place.

None of us know what's going to happen between now and this time tomorrow. An unexpected phone call in the middle of the night could change our lives. A destructive weapon could be unleashed somewhere in the world. We don't know what's going to happen to us personally, and we don't know what's going to happen to us globally. The word "happen" implies the unpredictability of life.

Paul used this word three times in chapter 1. In verse 12, he said, "Now I want you to know, brothers and sisters, that what has happened to me has actually served to advance the gospel." In verse 19 he declared that "what has happened to me will turn out for my deliverance." And in verse 27, he told the Philippians, "Whatever happens, conduct yourselves in a manner worthy of the gospel of Christ."

But what had happened to Paul? As I described in the first chapter of this book, all his plans had fallen apart and he was facing trial in Rome before Emperor Nero.

What has happened to you? Paul isn't the only person whose plans have fallen apart. He's not the only person who has faced hardship. We all have. Perhaps something has happened to you that has taken the wind out of your sails, the bounce out of your step, the twinkle out of your eye, and the joy out of your heart.

Well, that brings us to our next phrase: "What has happened to me has actually served."

Has Actually Served

The word "actually" is the Greek word *mallon*, which means "on the contrary," "rather," or "instead of." In other words, Paul was saying, "The things that have happened to me have—contrary to what people might think—turned out for good."

For example, suppose you said to me, "You must be very tired." I might reply, "*Actually* I feel great. I'm full of energy."

Similarly, Paul was saying, "People think what happened to me has hurt me and hindered the gospel, but *actually* the opposite has occurred."

What has happened to me has actually served. . . . That's an amazing word. What has happened to me—all of Paul's seeming misfortune and delay and imprisonment—all of that *actually* served. It's the same for the believer today. The circumstances of our lives have become servants of Christ's commands.

Our circumstances must bow before Jesus. We may not be able to control them, and chaos may seem to reign. But the Savior who turned water into wine and death into life can bring about a mutation, a transfiguration, a reversal, an evolution of our circumstances. The Savior can turn our circumstances into His servants for the advancement of His kingdom.

THE SAVIOR CAN TURN OUR CIRCUMSTANCES INTO HIS SERVANTS FOR THE ADVANCEMENT OF HIS KINGDOM.

This is part of redemption.

Mariana Laskava is a missionary to Ukraine with Word of Life. She works in a Bible institute near Kyiv and coaches students in evangelism. When the Russian invasion began, she had less than an hour to evacuate. She fled with only a small suitcase and ended up in Spain. She told a journalist:

> When you go into a storm like war, if you have a close relationship with God, you go through the storm holding on to something stable. . . . The emotions, the trauma that you go through can be very damaging, but if you hold on to God, the true strong tower, you can know the Lord even more. . . . In this storm, we have been able to bring the gospel to many people. In places where they have been left without homes, without resources, 90 percent of the volunteers working in Ukraine are Christians. The churches are filling up with people who don't know Christ. One church in Kiev that I know well is holding the meetings outside the church building because inside there is room for about eighty people and there are services where they have over three hundred attending. They are doing activities for children, for women. I have seen churches celebrating baptisms. So God is glorified even in the midst of the darkest hours of our country.[2]

That brings us to the last phrase of the sentence: "what has happened to me has actually served *to advance the gospel*" (emphasis mine).

To Advance the Gospel

That was all that was on Paul's mind—advancing the gospel. Paul talked about this many times, but really focused on it in this letter to the Philippians. The book has 104 verses, and the word *gospel* is used nine times. In terms of proportions and percentages, that's a greater concentration of the use of this word than in his other letters. The book of Romans is his only letter that uses the word more, but it has sixteen chapters.

In just the first chapter of this book, Paul mentioned the gospel six times: he partnered with the church in the spread of the gospel (v. 5); he was in chains for confirming the gospel (v. 7); he advanced the gospel (v. 12); he proclaimed the gospel (v. 14); he defended the gospel (v. 16); and he encouraged the Philippians to live in a manner worthy of the gospel, striving together as one in faith (v. 27).

When I see Paul's zeal here, I'm ashamed and ready to rededicate myself. How much does your zeal in life reflect Paul's concern for the advancement of the gospel?

How did what had happened to him—his adversity—serve to advance the gospel? In two ways. First, he was chained to soldiers twenty-four hours a day. He always seemed to be on good terms with the soldiers protecting him, and he shared his message with them. They were a captive audience—not only did he speak to them directly, but they heard his conversations with others and they listened as he prayed. He told the Philippians, "First of all, my imprisonment means a personal witness for Christ before the palace guards not to mention others who come and go" (1:13 PHILLIPS).

The imperial guard was made up of about ten thousand of Rome's best soldiers. They served under the direct command of Nero to protect him, to provide a police presence in Rome, and to do his bidding throughout the empire. Paul's converts among these soldiers took the gospel to far-flung regions he could never have gone himself.

What appeared to be Paul's tragedy was really God's strategy.

Second, Paul's circumstances had a bracing effect on the church. He said, "Most of our brothers, somehow taking fresh heart in the Lord from the very fact that I am a prisoner for Christ's sake, have shown far more courage in boldly proclaiming the Word of God" (Philippians 1:14 PHILLIPS).

We can see how this works, can't we? When you read of the courage of a Christian facing persecution in an oppressive land—when they stand bravely for Christ despite threats and intimidations—doesn't it encourage you to be bolder and more outspoken in your faith?

Gloomy thoughts come from the way we interpret the happenings of our lives. Paul knew that every single circumstance was under the providence, the sovereignty, and the control of Jesus Christ, who had turned an occupied tomb into an empty grave. He knew that everything worked together for the good of those who love God and are living according to His purposes. He could even see some of the benefits God was bringing about.

My friend John Murray told me of an experience he had while on a recent humanitarian missions trip to the Ivory Coast. He was with the Hanna Project, and they were doing medical work in the northeast of the country. One morning John woke up sick. He was so sick he decided he could not fulfill his duties that day. He had to stay in his temporary quarters. But while there in his quarters alone, an idea came to him for a sermon. The thoughts came to him so quickly that he got a legal pad and started writing them down. Soon the entire sermon was spread out before him. And then his strength and well-being returned, and the next day he resumed his work.

On the following Sunday he was surprised by an unexpected invitation to preach in one of the national churches. "Yes," he said, "I can preach. The Lord gave me a sermon while I was sick."

He went to the church, and his words were exactly what that church needed to hear. When he extended the invitation, twenty people responded to the appeal to receive Jesus Christ as their Lord and Savior. He said, "The Lord orchestrated the whole thing and even allowed my sickness in order for people to come to know His saving power."

In the light of the victory of Christ, John cast away his gloomy thoughts and replaced them with glorious ones.

We can do the same. The things that happen to us have a divine way of actually turning out for our good and for the furtherance of the gospel. In His own way and time, the Lord reverses adversity, overrides misfortune, and dismantles the devil's schemes.

He will do this for you.

Whatever happens, you can trust Him.

Chapter 8

WHATEVER HAPPENS . . .

ACCESS GOD'S PROVISION OF THE SPIRIT OF CHRIST

(PHILIPPIANS 1:18-19)

I've come across a phrase—a single phrase—that got into my bloodstream like an infusion and led me to much thought and soul-searching: *God's provision of the Spirit of Jesus Christ.*

The apostle Paul was under arrest in Rome, facing trial before Emperor Nero. If his trial was already in progress, he might have been in a holding cell near the royal courts. He was optimistic about the outcome:

> I rejoice. Yes, and I will continue to rejoice, for I know that through your prayers and God's provision of the Spirit of Jesus Christ what has happened to me will turn out for my deliverance. (Philippians 1:18–19)

Yes, and I Will Continue to Rejoice

The apostle Paul had made up his mind. No matter the outcome of his trial, he would be joyful. One of my most enduring pursuits has been the acquisition of biblical joy. I've studied this throughout Scripture, read about it, written about it, preached about it—and experienced it, though not as consistently as I should.

In my studies, I read a book that called joy a "high-energy state for the brain." The premise of the book is that the practice of joy endows us with the capacity to engage life with energy, creativity, and endurance. "High-joy people are very resilient," the author said. "High-joy communities are energetic and productive even in hard times. When we are empowered with joy, we are better able to suffer, withstand pain, and still maintain intact relationships."[1]

For I Know

How, then, do we become high-joy people? Joy comes from knowledge. Paul said: "Yes, and I will continue to rejoice, *for I know*" (emphasis mine). He knew something, and what he knew generated the electrical energy of his joy. A reality, a thought, an idea had come into his head. He had been pondering it, thinking about it, considering it. And the more he thought about it, the more joy he felt.

HOW, THEN, DO WE BECOME HIGH-JOY PEOPLE? JOY COMES FROM KNOWLEDGE. The same thing is true for us. Recently I let some things get to me and hurt me. The more I brooded over them, the lower I sank. I knew I had to get into a better state of mind, so I did that by going to Scripture and reminding myself of God's Word. The truth of Scripture, including the verses below, restored my joy.

- The precepts of the LORD are right, giving joy to the heart. (Psalm 19:8)
- Your statutes are my heritage forever; they are the joy of my heart. (Psalm 119:111)
- When your words came, I ate them; they were my joy and my heart's delight. (Jeremiah 15:16)

- [Jesus said,] "Remain in my love. . . . I have told you this so that my joy may be in you and that your joy may be complete." (John 15:9, 11)

We draw our shifting emotions from the things we *feel*, but we base our enduring attitudes on the things we *know*. So what did Paul know that brought him joy in the midst of his trials?

That Through Your Prayers

He knew the Philippians were praying for him. "I will continue to rejoice," he said, "for I know that *through your prayers*" (emphasis mine). How remarkable that this small congregation could lift Paul's name in prayer, and eight hundred miles away, strength and encouragement would enter his heart.

When I think of intercessory prayer—praying for others—I think of James O. Fraser, a missionary of yesteryear. When Fraser arrived in China at age twenty-two, he found lodgings in an attic room. Feeling lonely, he would rise each morning and go outside to hike in the fields and hills. There he prayed aloud, talking to God as to a friend. He often used a hymnbook, taking stanzas of the hymns and turning them into prayers. Sometimes he would pray for his city as he sat on the hilltop and looked down upon it.[2]

In his diary for March 13, 1916, Fraser wrote that he felt "much peace and rest of soul after making that definite prayer, and almost ecstatic joy."[3]

Follow his example. If you find yourself anxious and self-focused, tell yourself you must change the emphasis of your thoughts. Find a secret place and think of someone who needs prayer. Pace back and forth, talking to God about them earnestly. You'll suddenly recognize you're in God's presence, experiencing His fellowship as you plead for your friend (or enemy). In God's presence is fullness of joy (Psalm 16:11 NKJV), and the desolate mood of your mind will be broken up.

Like Fraser, I sometimes use a hymnbook in going about this. I remember singing a gospel song that said, "Send a

YOU'RE IN GOD'S PRESENCE, EXPERIENCING HIS FELLOWSHIP AS YOU PLEAD FOR YOUR FRIEND (OR ENEMY).

great revival in my soul. Let the Holy Spirit come and take control and send a great revival in my soul."[4]

I've prayed that song for others. "Lord, send a great revival to their soul. Let the Holy Spirit come and take control. Send a great revival to their soul."

The Philippians must have been praying something like that for Paul, and he believed God was altering his circumstances because of their prayers for him.

God's Provision of the Spirit of Jesus Christ

Now to the phrase that got into my bloodstream: "I will continue to rejoice, for I know that through your prayers *and God's provision of the Spirit of Jesus Christ*" (emphasis mine). The whole Trinity is in that phrase: *God's* provision of the *Spirit* of *Jesus Christ*.

Jesus Christ is the eternal God, the Son who has always existed and will always exist. But in coming to earth through a virgin's womb, He put aside many of the prerogatives of His God-ness. For example, as God, Jesus is omniscient. He knows absolutely everything about everything everywhere. But on earth in His humanity, Jesus "grew in wisdom" (Luke 2:52).

How, then, did Jesus know what to say? How did He do all He did?

Luke 3:21–22 says: "When all the people were being baptized, Jesus was baptized too. And as he was praying, heaven was opened and the Holy Spirit descended on him in bodily form like a dove. And a voice came from heaven: 'You are my Son, whom I love; with you I am well pleased.'"

Jesus was baptized, not only with water, but also with the Spirit. The Hebrew term *messiah* and the Greek title *Christ* both mean "Anointed One." The Father did His work through His Son by the Spirit, as these verses testify:

- "Very truly I tell you, the Son can do nothing by himself; he can do only what he sees his Father doing." (John 5:19)
- "For I did not speak on my own, but the Father who sent me

commanded me to say all that I have spoken. . . . Whatever I say is just what the Father has told me to say." (John 12:49–50)

- "The words I say to you I do not speak on my own authority. Rather, it is the Father, living in me, who is doing his work." (John 14:10)
- "These words you hear are not my own; they belong to the Father who sent me." (John 14:24)

The Father did His work and spoke His words through Jesus Christ. How? By the Holy Spirit.

Look at Luke 4:14–18:

"Jesus returned to Galilee in the power of the Spirit, and news about him spread through the whole countryside. . . . He went to Nazareth, where he had been brought up, and on the Sabbath day he went into the synagogue, as was his custom. He stood up to read, and the scroll of the prophet Isaiah was handed to him. Unrolling it, he found the place where it is written: 'The Spirit of the Lord is on me, because he has anointed me to proclaim good news to the poor.'"

In Matthew 12:28, Jesus declared, "It is by the Spirit of God that I drive out demons."

In Acts 10:38, Peter talked about "how God anointed Jesus of Nazareth with the Holy Spirit and power, and how he went around doing good and healing all who were under the power of the devil, because God was with him."

Just as God the Father baptized Jesus of Nazareth with the Spirit at the Jordan, so Jesus baptized His church with the Spirit on the day of Pentecost. As a result, just as God the Father did His work through His Son by His Spirit, so Jesus Christ does His work through us by His Spirit. As the Father spoke His words through the Son by the Spirit, so Jesus Christ speaks His words through us by His Spirit.

Major Ian Thomas, whose sermons, as I mentioned in chapter 6, have had a tremendous impact on my wife, Katrina, and me, once said: "In the upper room, Jesus told His disciples, 'I'm going back to the place from which I came, back to the One from whom I came—My Father—and because I am going back to My Father, the day will soon dawn when I, indwelling you by the same Holy Spirit through whom My Father now indwells Me, I will do through you the things My Father is now doing through Me.'"[5]

In his inimitable way, Major Thomas said: "When we as human beings make ourselves available to Jesus Christ in the same way that Jesus as man made Himself available to the Father, then Jesus will be to us in our humanity what the Father was to Him in His humanity. That is the whole Christian life in a nutshell."[6]

Thomas also said, "So the Christian life, of course, is the life that Christ lived then, lived now, by Him, in us. There is no other. And if your Christian life does not derive from that fact that Jesus Christ, risen from the dead, has come to take occupation of your humanity and become in you the origin of His own image and the source of His own activity and the dynamic of His own demands and the cause of His own effects, you've become a Christian but haven't yet learned to be one."[7]

That's why the epistles are full of teachings about the power offered by the Holy Spirit.

- "God's love has been poured out into our hearts through the Holy Spirit, who has been given to us." (Romans 5:5)
- "May the God of hope fill you with all joy and peace as you trust in him, so that you may overflow with hope by the power of the Holy Spirit." (Romans 15:13)
- "Do you not know that your bodies are temples of the Holy Spirit, who is in you, whom you have received from God? You are not your own." (1 Corinthians 6:19)
- "And we all, who with unveiled faces contemplate the Lord's glory, are being transformed into his image with ever-increasing glory, which comes from the Lord, who is the Spirit." (2 Corinthians 3:18)

This is what is meant by the provision of the Spirit. What a gift our God has given us!

What Has Happened to Me Will
Turn Out for My Deliverance

When the provision of the Spirit is combined with the prayers of the saints, it transforms all our circumstances. Paul concluded in Philippians 1:18–19, "I will continue to rejoice, for I know that through your prayers and God's provision of the Spirit of Jesus Christ *what has happened to me will turn out for my deliverance*" (emphasis mine).

The apostle Paul wasn't certain of how he would be delivered, but he knew it would be in one of two ways—either by his release or by his execution—and either was all right with him. We know this because he went on to say in verse 21, "For to me, to live is Christ and to die is gain."

We can have Paul's mindset, too, by following his example with these simple steps:

- Make up your mind to rejoice based on the knowledge you find in God's Word.
- Find someone who needs you to pray for them.
- Yield yourself to Christ and let Him fill you with His Spirit.

Remember—whatever happens, access God's provision of the Spirit of Christ.

Chapter 9

WHATEVER HAPPENS . . .

CHOOSE A LIFE MOTTO

(PHILIPPIANS 1:20-26)

Orison Swett Marden, a dejected orphan, found a book in an attic. The title was *Self-Help*, written by Scottish author Samuel Smiles. That book changed Marden's life. In the following years, Marden became America's first great motivational author, writing fifty books and founding *Success* magazine. In 1916, Marden wrote a book entitled *Getting the Most Out of Life*, and one of his chapters was "Choose a Life Motto," in which he wrote:

> The influence of an uplifting, energizing motto kept constantly in mind is invaluable. Multitudes of men and women owe their success in life to the daily inspiration of such a motto. . . . Who can estimate the value of a high ideal, crystalized in one uplifting sentence, constantly held in mind? . . . A life slogan which embodies your aim, stirs your ambition, and tends to arouse your latent potencies, will be worth infinitely more to you than an inherited fortune.[1]

Reading those words, I thought back to my college yearbook. The school asked graduating seniors to select a "life verse" to put under our pictures. I had so many verses, I asked if I could submit a life motto instead. They agreed. I still have my college yearbook, and there under my twenty-two-year-old self are these words: "The Will of God. Nothing More. Nothing Less."

That's a good motto and I've sought to live by it but I've since found another one. If I were graduating today, I would choose Philippians 1:21. It's the best motto I've ever heard. It fits any occasion and meets any moment. A dozen words, each of them only one syllable—yet they encompass anything and everything to which we could aspire.

For to me, to live is Christ and to die is gain.

That summarized Paul's philosophy and ordered his actions. It focused his aspirations and fueled his ambitions. It repressed his vices and regulated his conduct. Here's what he said in context:

> I eagerly expect and hope that I will in no way be ashamed, but will have sufficient courage so that now as always Christ will be exalted in my body, whether by life or by death. For to me, to live is Christ and to die is gain. If I am to go on living in the body, this will mean fruitful labor for me. Yet what shall I choose? I do not know! I am torn between the two: I desire to depart and be with Christ, which is better by far; but it is more necessary for you that I remain in the body. Convinced of this, I know that I will remain, and I will continue with all of you for your progress and joy in the faith, so that through my being with you again your boasting in Christ Jesus will abound on account of me. (Philippians 1:20–26)

As we've seen, the apostle was facing legal hearings before Emperor Nero concerning charges made nearly five years before in Jerusalem. He was constantly chained to soldiers, yet his attitude was strong, as we see in his six powerful affirmations.

I Eagerly Expect and Hope

The words *expect* and *hope* are synonyms that reflect a certainty. When the Bible talks about hope, it refers to total expectation and anticipation of something sure to happen. Paul was convinced God would give him sufficient courage regardless of any twists and turns in his legal turmoil.

Think of it. He was in a new situation, a threatening one he had never experienced before. He was about to stand in a Roman courtroom before the volatile ruler Nero and be called to account for his Christian faith. His emotional response to this challenge: "I do not expect to fall apart or have a spiritual breakdown or deny the faith. I do expect that God will give me sufficient courage so that whatever happens, I will exalt Christ—whether I'm set free or whether I'm executed" (my paraphrase).

> **I DO EXPECT THAT GOD WILL GIVE ME SUFFICIENT COURAGE SO THAT WHATEVER HAPPENS, I WILL EXALT CHRIST.**

I Will Have Sufficient Courage

I love the phrase "sufficient courage." It doesn't mean Paul didn't have anxious questions. But he was certain God would give him sufficient courage in the moment.

I recall many times when I would have collapsed if God had not given me sufficient courage. One of my first recollections is from when an elementary schoolmate said he was going to come to my house and beat me up. I'd never experienced bullying before, and I was scared. When he came, I lunged into him, grabbed him around the waist, hauled him to the ground, and we wrestled around for a little while. Not much came of it.

Looking back, I think I knew that if we got into a fistfight, I'd be in trouble. I had no idea how to use my fists. But if I could wrestle him to the ground, I'd have the advantage because I was what they called in those days "husky." That was the last time I had any trouble with him.

Since then, I've had many moments when I've wrestled with anxious fear. But looking back, God has always given me sufficient courage. He will give you sufficient courage too.

In *Pilgrim's Progress*, the travelers were frightened because they heard about two lions in the pathway ahead. But they trusted the Lord and pressed on.

Presently they found the lions on either side of the path, chained. Both roared and strained at their restraints, but there was just enough room for the travelers to pass between them unscathed. It took courage, though they were safe in the center of the pathway. In the same way, the Lord will give you sufficient courage for whatever you face on your pathway as you stay in the center of His will.

Christ Will Be Exalted Whatever Happens

The apostle Paul's courage embraced the fact that whatever happened—should he live or die—Christ would be exalted: "I . . . have sufficient courage so that now as always Christ will be exalted in my body, whether by life or by death."

When I was in college, I learned a song by Ray Hildebrand, a pop singer who became one of the earliest writers of contemporary Christian music. "If I Live Well, Praise the Lord" was my favorite song of his, and it ended with the words, "If I live or die, my only cry will be: Jesus in me, praise the Lord."

When you come to this point in your thinking, you're free to live with courage and confidence. Why? Because you're saying, "It doesn't matter what happens as long as Christ is exalted." You're repudiating the power of circumstances to affect the core of your life. You're disallowing the situations you face to determine the attitude you embrace. Whatever happens, it won't matter all that much as long as Christ is exalted in it all.

- I've studied for this examination, for this test, and I've done my best. If I pass it, praise the Lord. If I fail, praise the Lord. May He be exalted.
- I've worked hard for this promotion and I think I deserve it. If I get it, I will praise the Lord. If I don't, I'll praise Him anyway. May He be exalted.
- I want my mother to recover from her heart attack. If she does, praise the Lord. But if she doesn't—may Jesus Christ be praised.
- I'm facing the imperial judge because of my faith in Christ. If I'm released, praise the Lord. If I'm taken out and executed in the Circus Maximus, well, I will praise the Lord.

The attitude of exalting Christ whatever happens has the power to weaken or destroy the grip of circumstance-based anxiety in our lives—to live is Christ and to die is gain.

In the original Greek, this is very terse and alliterative. The word "Christ" is *Christos*. The word "gain" is *kerdos*. Paul was saying, "To live: Christos. To die: Kerdos."

Karen Ruth Johnson was a student about to graduate from San Marino High School in California. Her final assignment was to write a paper on her philosophy in life. She wrote it on Thursday night, gave it to her teacher on Friday, and on Saturday, she was killed in a head-on automobile collision. The tragedy set the tone for the class's graduation. Karen's diploma was awarded posthumously. Here is a portion of her final paper:

"My Philosophy of Life" by Karen Ruth Johnson

My philosophy of life is based on the Holy Bible and the God who wrote it. I know that He has a plan for my life and through daily prayer and reading of His Word I will be able to see it. As far as my life work or life partner I am leaving it in His hands.

I feel that this philosophy is very practical and can be applied to everyday life. Every decision can be taken to the Lord in prayer and the peace that comes from knowing Jesus Christ as my personal Savior is something many cannot understand. Many search for a purpose and reason for life. I know that I am on this earth to have fellowship with God and to win others to the saving knowledge of His Son, Jesus Christ. I know that after death I will go to be with Him forever. . . . Paul says in the New Testament, "Whatsoever ye do, do it all to the glory of God," and "For me, to live is Christ, to die is gain."

This is my philosophy, and yet it is not mine. But I am God's, and whatever I have is His. I have faith that He is the only answer and I do love Him so.[2]

May we all feel the same. May we, too, adopt this motto.

Here and now, the risen Christ, through the indwelling Holy Spirit, wants to be your Lord and your life, your Creator and Sustainer, your first thought

HE IS A FRIEND CLOSER THAN A BROTHER, RICHER THAN A TRILLIONAIRE, WISER THAN A SCHOLAR, GREATER THAN A RULER.

upon waking and your last thought before retiring. He should be the captivator of every motive and the motivator of every deed. He is a friend closer than a brother, richer than a trillionaire, wiser than a scholar, greater than a ruler. He came to give us life and to give it more abundantly. Paul said, in effect, "I want to know Him. He is my life."

Second Corinthians 5:15 says, "He died for all, that those who live should no longer live for themselves but for him who died for them and was raised again."

To Die Is Gain

Pressing further into our passage in Philippians, let's read verse 21: "For to me, to live is Christ and *to die is gain*" (emphasis mine). With this word and in the verses to follow, Paul painted a fourfold picture of the moment we die, or, rather, *depart* to be with Christ.

The word "gain"—*kerdos*—is used in the New Testament in reference to financial gain. If you invest a thousand dollars and make a hundred thousand on your investment, that's gain. It means to make a large profit. When we die, we come into an eternal life of divine dividends. In 2 Corinthians 12, Paul told of a vision in which he was caught up to heaven and given a glimpse of the heavenly inheritance that was awaiting him. It was beyond description. He knew death for him would be a gain.

I Desire to Depart and Be with Christ

Paul was not afraid of death. In Philippians 1:23, he said, "I am torn between [living and dying]: *I desire to depart*" (emphasis mine). Paul's use of "depart" was a nautical term. The Greeks used it to indicate raising the anchor and sailing from the harbor. Katrina and I took a cruise once. We flew to San Juan, Puerto Rico, showed up at the port, and I rolled her in her wheelchair onto the ship. We had a wonderful room, we heard the loud whistle blow, we felt the ship move, and we sat on the balcony and watched San Juan disappear as we traveled into the open sea, bound for some island. It was relaxing and idyllic.

That's the way Paul looked at death: "I desire to depart *and be with Christ*" (emphasis mine). He was ready to depart because he knew he would be with Christ. While we serve on earth, Christ lives within and around us by His Holy Spirit, but He Himself resides in heaven. The moment we depart for heaven, we're transported into the very presence of Jesus Himself, where we will see Him face-to-face, talk with Him person to person, enjoy Him friend to friend, and worship Him as servant to master. He told the Corinthian church that being absent from the body would mean he was present with the Lord (2 Corinthians 5:8).

To Be with Christ Is Far Better

Paul continued his explanation to the Philippians: "I desire to depart and be with Christ, *which is better by far*" (emphasis mine). It wasn't just better—it was better by far! Suppose you came to see me in the hospital where I was in constant pain and had a temperature of 104. You would say, "How are you?" And I would say, "I am languishing." A month later, you might call and ask again how I am. I would say, "I'm better. I'm at home. My fever and pain are gone, and I'm regaining my strength." Another month later, you would call to see how I am. "Oh," I'd say. "My family and I are driving down the Pacific Coast Highway in California, looking for a place to have supper while we watch the sunset. I am healed. I am well. I am vacationing. I am *better by far*." That's the language Paul was using. There is no superlative greater than that.

And that's why we can adopt as our motto: *To me, to live is Christ and to die is gain.*

I recently spoke to a very dear woman named Betty Byrd. She and her husband, Cecil, had served the Lord in Africa for many years. Their teenagers and a visiting intern were living there with them. On the night of January 20,

2000, after a game of Monopoly, the family headed for their beds. It was just another ordinary night in Mozambique.

Suddenly their son, Daniel, burst into the bedroom. "Mom, Mom," he cried. "Did you hear those gunshots?" As he spoke, four bandits with AK-47s entered the house, shot Cecil in the chest, killing him, and forced Daniel to escort them from the area. Thankfully they let Daniel live.

Betty recalled that in the days that followed, Philippians 1:21 acquired fresh meaning for her. "I claimed it," she told me. "'For to me, to live is Christ; to die is gain.' The death part was for my husband; I knew he had gained. While he was on earth, he very much said, 'to live is Christ.' But the Lord took him, and that was his gain. The living part was now for me, and I was determined to make life worth living. Christ was and is my motivation. God would not let me give up."

As I researched her story a bit more, I found a transcript of a podcast that featured her testimony. In it, Betty says that she is not the same person she was before her husband died. She's stronger. Braver. And even more joyful.

"I think I am more outspoken. I have a little bit more courage," Betty reflected. "I don't even know how to say this, but in some ways, I have more joy. I've always been a happy person and felt the peace and joy of Jesus in my life, but I just feel my joy growing and growing and growing even in these seventeen years since Cecil's death."

One day while speaking at a convention in Atlanta, Betty was praying about her grief. She had her Bible open and noticed the verse in Nehemiah that said, "The joy of the LORD is your strength" (Nehemiah 8:10). And then she noticed something she hadn't seen before.

"Just before it says, 'The joy of the LORD is your strength,' it says, 'Do not grieve.' I had never thought about that before. From that day forth, I thought, Okay, there is a time to grieve, but now is the time for grieving to be ended and to let the joy of the Lord be my strength. And now, He just keeps increasing it."[3]

Let's have a relationship with Christ like that—one so meaningful we can say with all our hearts: "Whether I live or whether I die, my song shall be: Jesus is with me. Praise the Lord!"

Chapter 10

WHATEVER HAPPENS . . .

NEVER BE INTIMIDATED

(PHILIPPIANS 1:27-30)

Whathat do you do when persecution is so great you can no longer live in your own nation? In *100 Bible Verses that Made America*, I wrote about a church in England during the days of King James I. The persecution was so sustained, the entire church voted to immigrate to Holland, where there was more liberty. Some of those members would later go a step further and immigrate to America, still seeking religious liberty. We call them the Pilgrims.

The same persecution is happening today. According to *Voice of the Martyrs* in 2022, a church of about seventy believers in China faced so much pressure that some of the members suggested moving out of the country. Fifty-three members voted to leave and seventeen opposed. Sixty people ended up moving to an island belonging to South Korea, but things there haven't gone well. None of them spoke the Korean language, so instead of the high-paying, professional jobs they had in China, they had to take menial, backbreaking work. Further, South Korea is too afraid of China to extend asylum to the believers. These Christians simply do not know what to do.[1]

What do we do in circumstances like these? What would you do? Even in

America, Christians are facing increasing discrimination. We can find the best advice for this situation in Philippians 1:27–30. These verses begin the actual body, or *corpus*, of the letter.

Paul spent the first twenty-six verses of Philippians greeting the Philippians, thanking God and praying for them, then telling them about his circumstances and his resulting attitude. Now he was ready to get down to business. The core—the corpus, the essence, the backbone—of Philippians goes from Philippians 1:27 to Philippians 4:1. Everything we've studied so far has simply prepared us for the message that begins here in the last four verses of chapter 1.

> Whatever happens, conduct yourselves in a manner worthy of the gospel of Christ. Then, whether I come and see you or only hear about you in my absence, I will know that you stand firm in the one Spirit, striving together as one for the faith of the gospel without being frightened in any way by those who oppose you. This is a sign to them that they will be destroyed, but that you will be saved—and that by God. For it has been granted to you on behalf of Christ not only to believe in him, but also to suffer for him, since you are going through the same struggle you saw I had, and now hear that I still have (Philippians 1:27–30).

Our Two Problems

In his commentary on this passage, theologian Dr. Gordon Fee wrote, "[This whole] paragraph is a single, nearly impossible, sentence in Greek, which probably assumes this form because Paul tries to include all the urgencies of the letter . . . in this opening word."[2]

In other words, the rest of the book of Philippians is simply the unpacking of what Paul initially stated in this paragraph. I believe verse 27 is the key to the entire book: "Whatever happens, conduct yourselves in a manner worthy of the gospel of Christ. Then . . . I will know that you stand firm."

We have seen that Paul and the Philippians had two problems, and even after two thousand years, those problems have not disappeared. They are still frustrating us today.

First, we face opposition. Still, Paul said we should not be "frightened in any way by those who oppose you. This is a sign to them that they will be destroyed." We're facing opposition in this world from people who will be destroyed in the future. Dictators are not going to live forever. One day God will strike them down and judge the evil in their hearts.

Second, we are facing uncertainty. As indicated earlier, the phrase "whatever happens" is an admission that we don't know what's going to happen from day to day. Paul didn't know what was going to happen to him either.

Our One Responsibility

That brings us to our great responsibility: We are to conduct ourselves *worthy of the gospel*. The Greek text conveys the idea to live as a worthy citizen. The Christian Standard Bible translates this verse: "As citizens of heaven, live your life worthy of the gospel of Christ."

Philippi was an unusual city in the Roman world. Shortly before the birth of Christ, the Roman Republic was torn apart by civil war. About two hundred thousand men gathered just west of Philippi. The story is too long to tell, but in the aftermath of it all, Octavian, who emerged as emperor, granted Roman citizenship to the city of Philippi. Citizenship came with many benefits. The Philippians were proud and blessed to be citizens of the empire.

For the Christians in Paul's time, however, it was a mixed blessing. The city had an obligation to cheer Emperor Nero as their lord (*kurios*) at every civic gathering and athletic event. To Christians, only Christ was *kurios*—Lord. On two occasions in this letter—here and in Philippians 3:20—Paul reminded them—and us—that we are citizens of the everlasting kingdom. Our heavenly citizenship is our primary citizenship. We are citizens of heaven who are traveling through earth, who happen to hold an American passport or a British passport or whatever we have.

In other words, we are expatriates—citizens of one nation living in another that is not our own. As a result, we have three obligations.

> **WE ARE EXPATRIATES—CITIZENS OF ONE NATION LIVING IN ANOTHER THAT IS NOT OUR OWN.**

Our Three Obligations

Lots of people today are more focused on their *rights* than on their *obligations* as citizens. Sometimes I'm one of them. I chafe at having to keep the speed limit, fulfill jury duty, or pay taxes. But if I think my freedom of speech is endangered, I'll crusade to be heard.

When it comes to our heavenly citizenship, our privileges are limitless, but we also have responsibilities.

Stand Firm in One Spirit

First, we're to stand firm in one Spirit: "Whatever happens, conduct yourselves in a manner worthy of the gospel of Christ. Then . . . *I will know that you stand firm in the one Spirit*" (emphasis mine).

I want to tell you about a rosebush I've just planted. A woman in New Orleans named Peggy Martin had a beautiful garden of four hundred and fifty roses. One was an old garden rose she couldn't identify. No one knew the name or background of this vigorous climbing rose.

In August 2005, Hurricane Katrina struck New Orleans, and Peggy's garden was covered by twenty feet of contaminated water. All her roses perished except for the one that had no name. It came back stronger than ever—and the rose experts named it the Peggy Martin. That's its official name. But it's better known by its nickname—the Katrina rose.

My wife's name was Katrina. During the storm, she said, "My name has never been mentioned in prayer as often as now." Well, you can see why I ordered a Katrina rose and have set it out in my garden.

I want to be like that rose—to stand firm, to thrive even when engulfed, even if there's an ocean of opposition against me, even if the winds blow and the tides rise, and even if the contaminated world tries to marginalize and vilify me. I want to remain rooted, grounded, and resilient. I'm sure you do too.

That happens by the Holy Spirit who is within us. We're to stand firm in one Spirit. The secret of the Katrina rose is its vintage sap, the circulating fluid that gave it a near-supernatural sort of energy and vitality. But that's nothing compared to the Spirit-filled power of the Spirit-filled follower of Christ.

Stand firm in one Spirit.

Strive Together for One Faith

Second, we conduct ourselves as citizens of heaven when we strive together for one faith: "Whatever happens, conduct yourselves in a manner worthy of the gospel of Christ. Then . . . I will know that you stand firm in the one Spirit, *striving together as one for the faith of the gospel*" (emphasis mine).

The phrase "striving together" comes from the Greek term *athlos*, from which we get our English word *athletics*. The apostle Paul often used sports and athletic metaphors. He talked about running the race or wrestling in prayer.

A year or so ago, I had a speaking engagement that was seven hours away by car. A month or so earlier, I had contracted COVID. I was over the illness, but not over the fatigue. I awoke Saturday morning, so tired and weary that I thought, *I cannot possibly make this trip. I don't feel like driving to the grocery store, let alone to my appointment.*

I tried to figure out how to get out of the engagement, but I knew people were counting on me. I got in my truck, pulled onto the interstate, and drove to the first rest stop. There, I took a nap. Then I drove to the next rest stop and did the same. By stopping and napping at every rest stop, I was able to get to my hotel by the end of the day.

Later, on a call with Dr. David Jeremiah about a totally different subject, we began talking about our travels. I told him about the experience, and he looked over at his wife, Donna, and said, "Who does something like that?"

"You do," Donna replied.

"Well, yes, we all do. We all do. That's called ministry."

Just like an athletic contest, living "worthy of the gospel of Christ" takes endurance. We're striving together for the faith without being intimidated by our opponents. Many Western Christians are caught in a triangle of trepidation. We don't speak up because we're afraid we'll come across as harsh and intolerant; we're afraid we'll hurt or offend someone; or we're afraid we'll be criticized, rejected, or attacked.

I know what it's like to speak as lovingly as I know how about the sanctity of gender, sexuality, and marriage—only to have my own friends question whether I should have brought up the subject.

None of us want to be harsh, hurt, or hunted. But our silence isn't doing the world any good. The Lord tells us here to always be "striving together as one for the faith of the gospel without being frightened in any way by those who oppose you."

Suffer for One Cause

That may lead to suffering, but that's all right. The passage anticipates that. Conducting ourselves as citizens of heaven while in this hostile environment means standing firm in one spirit, striving together for one faith, and suffering for one cause.

Verse 29 can't say it any clearer: "For it has been granted to you on behalf of Christ not only to believe in him, but also to suffer for him."

For the Philippians and for Paul, some suffering was caused by persecution. But there are also the inevitable sufferings of life. None of us like that word, *suffering*, and when we see it in the Bible it often makes us shrink back a bit.

Recently, however, I've been reading in two Old Testament books—Deuteronomy and Isaiah. And I've found the same truth in both books: Our Lord carries us.

- "You saw how the LORD your God carried you, as a father carries his son, all the way you went until you reached this place." (Deuteronomy 1:31)
- "Listen to me . . . you whom I have upheld since your birth, and have carried since you were born." (Isaiah 46:3)

I had lunch with a couple of friends not long ago, and I told them how much this had been true for me over my life. The Lord has carried me, especially across the rough places. One of my friends said, "Yes, and when God carries us, we have only one obligation."

"What is it?" I asked.

"To hold on."

I'd never thought of that. God carries us through times of suffering, yes. But we must hold on to Him, arms around His neck, as it were, by faith. Of course, we don't have to hold on—God can carry us without any effort on our own, but we don't always allow Him to do so. Like a toddler being picked up by his father, we can either rest or (as many toddlers do) resist and push away.

One of the most gripping books I've read is pastor Andrew Brunson's account of his 735-day ordeal in Turkish prisons because of his work for Christ. I've not met Brunson, but he attended a couple of schools after me, and I have utmost respect for him. When Turkey's President Erdogan had Brunson arrested in 2016, it began a harrowing period. Brunson writes about his fear, the psychological torture he endured, the gripping anxiety and panic he felt, and how he thought he was losing his mind.

GOD CARRIES US THROUGH TIMES OF SUFFERING, YES. BUT WE MUST HOLD ON TO HIM.

He clung to the neck of Jesus, but sometimes he feared the Lord would drop him. At times Brunson wasn't sure he would survive or that he would stand for Christ when the moment came. When his case finally came up for trial, he was in as much peril as Paul when he wrote Philippians—maybe more. He was terrified. But God gave him grace, and when he rose to speak, this is what he said in the courtroom and to the government and to all of Turkey:

> Jesus told His disciples to go to all the world and proclaim the good news of salvation to everyone and make disciples. This is why I came to Turkey—to proclaim this.
>
> There is only one way to God: Jesus. There is only one way to have our sins forgiven: Jesus. There is only one way to gain eternal life: Jesus. There is only one Savior: Jesus. I want this to echo in all of Turkey.[3]

It did. And it will.

These are the most dangerous days we have ever faced. There's opposition and uncertainty. But there is grace for the moment—grace for the standing, grace for the struggling, and grace for the suffering. We are being carried through it all, and we simply need to hold on to our Savior in faith and confidence . . . whatever happens.

Chapter 11

WHATEVER HAPPENS . . .

MAKE TODAY ABOUT OTHERS

(PHILIPPIANS 2:1-5)

Problems in the royal family—it's what keeps tabloids going. And book publishers. And talk shows. You could spend your entire year just reading the books that have been published, for example, about two brothers whose names happen to be William and Harry. It's sad when the king's kids can't get along.

The King of kings has a family on earth, too, and He doesn't want us to be in tumult with one another. He wants us to get along, to love one another, and to operate with a sense of unity, humility, and love. But that's a challenge for us. As a pastor for decades, I've learned a lot about unity and disunity in a church or home. It's been a challenge from the very beginning—from New Testament days. How do we maintain sweet unity among Christians?

The apostle Paul addressed this throughout the book of Philippians, and especially as he began the second chapter of his letter:

Therefore if you have any encouragement from being united with Christ, if any comfort from his love, if any common sharing in the Spirit, if any tenderness and compassion, then make my joy complete by being like-minded, having the same love, being one in spirit and of one mind. Do nothing out of selfish ambition or vain conceit. Rather, in humility value others above yourselves, not looking to your own interests but each of you to the interests of the others. In your relationships with one another, have the same mindset as Christ Jesus. (Philippians 2:1–5)

Trinity

The first word of chapter 2, *therefore*, links this paragraph to the preceding one, where Paul said, "Whatever happens, conduct yourselves in a manner worthy of the gospel of Christ. Then, whether I come and see you or only hear about you in my absence, I will know that you stand firm in the one Spirit" (Philippians 1:27).

Moving on, Paul told the Philippians to expect trouble in this world, but to stand firm and united. Since they had the spiritual resources that come from the Trinity—the encouragement of Jesus, the love of God the Father, and the fellowship of the Holy Spirit—they could draw on them for success.

Dr. Gordon Fee, in his commentary on the book of Philippians, suggests that Paul was using the same trinitarian formula he used in 2 Corinthians 13:14: "May the grace of the Lord Jesus Christ, and the love of God, and the fellowship of the Holy Spirit be with you all."[1]

Since we have the grace, union, and encouragement of Jesus Christ and since we have the bottomless ocean of God's love and since we have the presence and power of the Holy Spirit, then we should be able to have good relationships. These invisible, innermost resources from heaven ought to energize us.

When my dad was born in the Tennessee mountains in 1911, there was no electricity. It wasn't until the 1930s and '40s that electricity came to parts of East Tennessee. I wish I had asked my dad about the first time he experienced a light switch. I read about one man who was so excited he scurried from room to room in his house turning the lights on and off. He was crying one minute and laughing the next. He looked at his wife, who was crying, and said, "Ain't it wonderful."[2]

One woman told me she and her siblings slept together in the sheer darkness of the attic. Their father would lead them up the steps with the coal-oil lamp, see that they were safely tucked in, and there they would stay in blackness until the sun rose. When electricity came, their father no longer led them up the steps and they were no longer in darkness. She missed the nostalgia of those days but didn't want to go back to them.

That's how it is when we discover the grace of our Lord Jesus Christ, the love of God, and the fellowship of the Holy Spirit. Suddenly we have light. We have power. We have warmth. We're connected to the divine transformers of the Trinity—and that makes an irreversible change in our lives. We can hear music from far away. We can view the world with new insight. We are electrified by heaven.

Unity

Paul went on to say in verse 2 that, since we have these resources of the triune God, we should be "like-minded, having the same love, being one in spirit and of one mind."

This doesn't mean we all have the same opinions about everything. It means that, since we have the same opinions about the essential things, we can have more patience with what is nonessential. The great British pastor and hymnist John Newton put it all together like this:

> *May the grace of Christ our Savior*
> *and the Father's boundless love,*
> *with the Holy Spirit's favor,*
> *rest upon us from above.*
> *Thus may we abide in union*
> *with each other and the Lord,*
> *and possess in sweet communion*
> *joys which earth cannot afford.*[3]

Love this

It often confuses people when they discover that Christian homes, families, churches, schools, mission agencies, and organizations are full of people who have trouble getting along with each other. It's a problem that goes all the way back to the bickering of the disciples in the Gospels, and to the argument between Paul and Barnabas in the book of Acts.

There are two reasons for it. First, Christians are people of deep convictions. We're committed to what we know and believe. Second, we are a diverse group of people. In every church, for example, people come from different backgrounds with different levels of maturity and with diverse opinions. Not every believer is spiritually mature. Some are babes in Christ while others who think they are mature are truly not.

That's why we have to work so hard on being of one spirit. I'll give you an example. I've been a member of the same denomination for seven decades. I was born into it. My grandfather was a preacher in this denomination, and my father

WE HAVE TO WORK SO HARD ON BEING OF ONE SPIRIT.

was the assistant clerk for our national association. So I began going to our annual meetings when I was a child. By the time I became a pastor and began attending as a delegate, things were very tense. There were a lot of arguments. There were divisive cliques.

Somehow over the years it seems we've learned how much that wears us down. Maybe it helped that some people left, but the rest of us—including me—decided that having an encouraging, cooperative spirit was much better than fighting.

The same thing happened once in my own church. Midway through my ministry, a terrible argument arose that lasted nearly a year and just about sent me to the grave. Maybe it helped that some people left, but the rest of us—including me—decided that having an encouraging, cooperative spirit was much better than fighting.

Humility

But that requires something. It requires us to learn to be humble. Paul went on to say in verses 3 and 4, "Do nothing out of selfish ambition or vain conceit.

Rather, in humility value others above yourselves, not looking to your own interests but each of you to the interests of the others."

This is Paul's version of the Golden Rule that Jesus gave us. Love is being more concerned about someone else's needs than about your own.

The easiest way to become a humble person is to begin acting like one. I don't mean to do it artificially. Nor do I mean to run yourself down and adopt or develop an inferiority complex—that's not humility.

But humility takes practice. If someone cuts in front of you on the highway to get into your lane, tap your brakes and let them in. When someone wants to talk to you, give them your full attention without looking at your phone. When you and your spouse go out to eat, let the other person's wishes prevail. When you enter the restaurant, hold the door and let the other person enter first. Be pleasant to your server and leave a generous tip. If you stop at the grocery store on the way home, return the shopping cart to the rack.

I read about someone who happened to see a famous man washing his hands in the public restroom. The observer was amazed that the man took pains to use paper towels to clean up the sink and dry off the counter before he left.

My favorite quote about humility is this one that I wrote down in my notebook while in college: "Humility is not thinking less of yourself. It's not thinking of yourself at all—and of Jesus more and more."

My friends—since we have the grace of the Lord Jesus Christ in our lives and the love of God and the fellowship of the Holy Spirit, since we've been electrified and energized, since we've gotten light and warmth and power—let's be tender and compassionate to one another in our marriages, homes, churches, communities. Let's be like-minded and of one heart and spirit. Let's do nothing through selfish ambition or vain conceit, but in lowliness of mind be more concerned about the other person than about ourselves. Let's have the mind of Christ.

On this hostile earth, the King's kids need to stick together.

ON THIS HOSTILE EARTH, THE KING'S KIDS NEED TO STICK TOGETHER.

Chapter 12

WHATEVER HAPPENS . . .

CULTIVATE THE MIND OF CHRIST

(PHILIPPIANS 2:6-11)

O pinions. Everyone has them. We all have a lot of opinions about a lot of things. And we've never had more ways of sharing them. Billions of people sharing trillions of opinions in quadrillions of ways.

And most of them are wrong. Just because someone is sincere, thoughtful, and intelligent—doesn't mean their every opinion is correct. I think mine are correct, of course; if I didn't I would change them, right? But I've lived long enough to know I'm not *always* right.

How about you? Do you sometimes find yourself clinging to your opinions out of sheer stubbornness? That's a common human trait. Only one person thinks correctly about every issue all the time—infallibly, unfailingly. In Isaiah 55, the Lord Almighty said: "For my thoughts are not your thoughts, neither are your ways my ways. . . . As the heavens are higher than the earth, so are my ways higher than your ways and my thoughts than your thoughts" (Isaiah 55:8–9).

God's omniscience and truthfulness merge with infinite brilliance. He knows everything, and every word He speaks is true. There are no mistakes in His thinking and no confusion in His mind. He has revealed some of His thoughts to us through Scripture. The passage in Isaiah continues: "As the rain and the snow come down from heaven, and do not return to it without watering the earth and making it bud and flourish, so that it yields seed for the sower and bread for the eater, so is my word that goes out from my mouth: It will not return to me empty" (Isaiah 55:10–11).

Only by taking our Bible in our hands and studying it, pondering it, and meditating on its verses can we begin to see and understand the world as God does. Only as we understand love and life and relationships from His perspective can we experience love and life and relationships that are healthy and whole.

There's a New Testament phrase for this—*the mind of Christ*. It's found in one of the most glorious passages in Paul's writings. Many people believe it's a song, likely one Paul composed to teach people the true nature of Jesus Christ. It begins, "Let this mind be in you which was also in Christ Jesus" (Philippians 2:5 NKJV).

The word "mind" comes from the Greek term *phroneo*, which occurs several times in Philippians. For example, in chapter 3, verse 15, Paul said, "All of us, then, who are mature should take such a view of things." The phrase "view of things" is the same word as "mind" in 2:5.

Wisdom is having a view of things that mirrors the thoughts of God; it's thinking about things as Christ does. We should see one another (spouse, sibling, child, parent, boss, coach, friend, enemy) with the same attitude as Jesus has toward us. I wish I always reflected the thoughts of Jesus. When I do, I'm always in the right; when I don't, I'm always in the wrong. Oh, how I long for you and me to grow in the wisdom that belongs to Christ Jesus. We need to think of ourselves as He does. What He thinks of us is revealed in the history of His life, in the story of what He has done.

WISDOM IS HAVING A VIEW OF THINGS THAT MIRRORS THE THOUGHTS OF GOD

In explaining this, Paul presented four great phases of the life of Jesus Christ. They demonstrate the cycle of Christ's redemptive career.

Christ's Preexistence

Philippians 2:6 says: "Who, being in very nature God." According to this declarative verse, Jesus Christ was, is, and always will be, in His very nature,

God. He is God Himself. The word "nature" is the Greek *morphe*, from which we get our word "morphology," a branch of biology devoted to the essential nature of living beings. According to Philippians 2:6, Jesus is, in His essential being, the almighty, eternal God.

This is why I'm bemused when people claim the notion of the deity of Christ was invented by the Council of Nicaea in AD 325. No. It was articulated there, but here in Philippians, two hundred and fifty years before the Council of Nicaea, Paul described Jesus as being in very nature or essence—*morphe*—God. The teaching of the deity of Jesus Christ cascades like a massive system of waterfalls, flowing through the Bible. The entire message of the Bible depends on it.

And thank goodness it does. If Jesus were anyone less than Almighty God, we could never find in Him the ultimate help, comfort, pardon, and eternity we crave.

Christ's Incarnation

Yet being God, Jesus "did not consider equality with God something to be used to his own advantage; rather, he made himself nothing by taking the very nature of a servant, being made in human likeness" (vv. 6–7).

Jesus didn't just come in the form of a man. He *became* a man. He became human. The New Living Translation says, "Though he was God, he did not think of equality with God as something to cling to. Instead, he gave up his divine privileges; he took the humble position of a slave and was born as a human being."

In His essence, His nature, and His eternal attributes, He was equal with God and was God. But in His infinite love and humility, He did not take undue advantage of His position. He didn't want His God nature to keep Him from doing something redemptive. He didn't want the glory of His throne to keep Him from the duty of His mission.

Verse 7 is one of the greatest mysteries of Scripture: "He made himself nothing." Some translations say He "emptied himself." No one fully understands this.

The word "nothing" comes from the Greek word *kenosis*, and this passage is known among scholars as the "Kenosis Passage." In simple language, God the Son stripped off the prerogatives and privileges of His glorious throne. He stepped away from heaven to enter human history. There is no evidence that Jesus stopped being God; indeed, that would be a rational impossibility. God cannot stop being God. But He emptied Himself of His privileges and prerogatives, temporarily abdicating heaven's throne to enter human history through the womb of a virgin.

He did not empty Himself of His *deity*, but temporarily of His *glory*. He took upon Himself the nature of a servant. He has always possessed His divine nature, but now He added to it. He took on something new. He assumed a new nature. According to Philippians 2, Jesus now had two natures.

You and I only have one nature. We only have one substance, one essence of who we are. We are humans. We are not humans and insects. We are not humans and angels. We are certainly not humans and gods as some religions suggest.

But Jesus, who is in very nature God, took upon Himself the additional nature of a servant. He did not simply become a God who appeared in a human body. He actually became a human person with a human body. There are two great incomprehensible mysteries at the heart of Christianity: (1) the Trinity—one God in three persons; and (2) the duality—one Man with two natures.

A GOD SMALL ENOUGH TO BE UNDERSTOOD IS NOT BIG ENOUGH TO BE WORSHIPPED.

We can explain it to a point. But beyond that point, it boggles our minds, as it should. As Evelyn Underhill said, "If God were small enough to be understood, He would not be big enough to be worshipped." Charles Wesley put it like this:

He left His Father's throne above,
So free, so infinite His grace,
Emptied Himself of all but love,
And died for Adam's helpless race;
'Tis mercy all, immense and free;
For, O my God, it found out me.[1]

Christ's Crucifixion

The passage continues: "He . . . was born as a human being. When he appeared in human form, he humbled himself in obedience to God and died a criminal's death on a cross" (Philippians 2:7–8 NLT).

The cross was the most repulsive form of execution ever invented. From the heavenly throne to the anguishing cross—no one but Jesus has ever made a journey like that. And He did it for you and for me.

Back in 2015, a Bolivian politician named Edwin Tupa wanted to run for mayor of his town. Unfortunately, he was a former congressman and Bolivian law banned national politicians from running in local races. That frustrated Tupa so much he staged a hunger strike. When that didn't work, he did the most dramatic thing you can imagine.

He said he was going to let himself be crucified in front of the Electoral Tribunal Building in La Paz. The news media gathered along with a large crowd. Tupa stretched himself out on a cross, but the crucifixion didn't get very far. As soon as one twelve inch nail was hammered into his right hand, he screamed in intense pain and begged his supporters to stop. He passed out, and it took paramedics ten minutes to remove the nail from his hand.[2]

Jesus offered both His hands and His feet to the nails. He offered His back to be scourged. He offered His brow to the thorns, His side to the spear, His clothes to His tormentors, His mother to His disciple, and His life's blood for all of us. Why?

God created us in His image to live with Him forever. Our personal failures separate us from Him. So God Himself, through the second person of the Trinity, descended into this world to die for our sins. He offered Himself as a sacrifice to atone for our sins, becoming obedient to death on the cross.

Christ's Exaltation

Verses 9–11 bring the story full circle: "Therefore God exalted him to the highest place and gave him the name that is above every name, that at the name of Jesus every knee should bow, in heaven and on earth and under the earth, and every tongue acknowledge that Jesus Christ is Lord, to the glory of God the Father."

In Jesus, we see the humblest Man who ever lived exalted to the highest place ever conceived. One day every tongue will acknowledge Him—those in heaven (all the angelic hosts), everyone on earth (all the humans), and everyone under the earth, which is the cosmic location of the demonic spirits.

Likewise, our future exaltation will be in reverse proportion to our current humility.

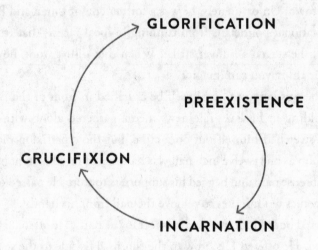

Years ago, I was teaching a teen camp in New York State. One day I asked the young people to answer the question: "Who is Jesus Christ?" As I read their answers later that day, I was intrigued by their diverse understanding of Christ, but one answer in particular has stayed with me all these years. A teenaged boy wrote these words: "Who is Jesus Christ? He is the God who made my relationship with my dad peaceful and meaningful."

That young man knew two things about Christ. First, he knew that Jesus is God. Second, he knew that Jesus has the power to change our lives and our relationships. That young man knew more about Jesus Christ than many of the millions who crowd into church every Sunday. Jesus is God, and He has the power to change our lives and our relationships.

Dr. Harold J. Sala, a pioneer in Christian radio, has many stories that have been told and retold. On one of his broadcasts, he mentioned his friend Doug Nichols, who worked in India. Doug had contracted tuberculosis and was sent to a sanitarium to recuperate. His fellow patients thought he was a rich American and wanted little to do with him. They didn't realize he was just as impoverished as they were. Doug tried to tell them about Jesus and offer them literature, but they politely refused.

One morning, Doug noticed an old man trying to sit on the edge of the bed, but because of weakness he fell backward and started sobbing. Soon a stench wafted from his bed. The old man was unable to get to the bathroom.

Doug recalled, "The nurses were extremely agitated and angry because they had to clean up the mess. One of the nurses in her anger even slapped him. The man, terribly embarrassed, just curled up into a ball and wept."

The next morning about 2:00 a.m., Doug noticed the old man trying to get himself out of bed again. Doug got up, went over to him, put one arm around his neck and the other under his legs. Then he gently carried him to the bathroom. When the man finished, Doug carried him back to his bed.

The old man, speaking a language Doug didn't understand, thanked him profusely and kissed his cheek. Doug went back to bed and fell asleep, but the next morning he awoke to a steaming cup of tea served by another patient, who motioned he would like some of Doug's literature.

"Throughout the day," Doug said, "people came to me, asking for the gospel booklets. This included the nurses, the hospital interns, the doctors, until everyone in the hospital had a tract, booklet, or Gospel of John. Over the next few days, several indicated they had trusted Christ as Savior as a result of reading the good news."[3]

The world doesn't care much about our opinions; they need men and women who have the mind, the heart, the attitude, the humility of Christ. "I simply took an old man to the bathroom," said Doug. "Anyone could have done that."

Anyone can, but not everyone does.

It takes someone with the mind of the Man of Galilee—Jesus Christ.

Chapter 13

WHATEVER HAPPENS . . .

WORK *OUT* WHAT GOD WORKS *IN*

(PHILIPPIANS 2:12-13)

This year I replaced some old carpet in my house. When the installers came, they pulled me aside and showed me a wet spot on the floor. "You must have a leak," they said. "It's coming from the heating and air-conditioning unit."

I called the air-conditioning and heating people, who came out and inspected the problem. "It's not us," they said. "It's from the pipes from the powder room. You'll have to call a plumber." I called the plumbing company, and the young man came out and said, "Yes, I can fix the problem. But you'd better sit down while I give you the estimate."

It wasn't a cheap repair, and it wasn't in a noticeable spot, in a utility closet behind a bunch of pipes and ductwork. But there, in the corner of a dark closet, was a serious problem that needed fixing.

We need interior maintenance too.

On the outside things may seem glamorous or glorious, but inside us, a leak in a closet or a short circuit in the wiring awaits repair. I can recommend a divine plumber, a flawless electrician, an unseen handyman who delights in working in the interior of our lives. Paul addressed this in Philippians 2:12–13:

Therefore, my dear friends, as you have always obeyed—not only in my presence, but now much more in my absence—continue to work out your salvation with fear and trembling, for it is God who works in you to will and to act in order to fulfill his good purpose.

In other words, if we have the grace of Jesus Christ, the love of God, and the fellowship of the Holy Spirit electrifying us, then we should be more concerned for other people than we are for ourselves.

Take Jesus Christ as an example. Though He was in His very essence God, He didn't cling to His position when it came to meeting our needs. We should follow His example in humility and work out in real life what He is working into us day by day.

This doesn't mean we can work *for* our salvation, but we can work *out* our salvation. We can *work out* what God is *working into* us. Let's look at the two sides of this.

God Is Working Inside You

If you're a follower of Christ, God is working inside you. The Greek here is *energeo*, from which we get our word *energy*. God is working within you with His divine energy. I want to talk about six New Testament passages that tell how the Lord operates in the interior of our lives: Philippians 1:6; Colossians 1:29; 2 Thessalonians 2:13; 1 Thessalonians 2:13; Hebrews 13:20–21; and Ephesians 3:20–21.

First, *God works inside us from the day we respond to the gospel.* For the Philippians, that went back to the day Paul, Silas, Luke, and Timothy arrived in northeastern Greece and began preaching the gospel. Remember Philippians 1:6: "He who began a good work in you will carry it on to completion until the day of Christ Jesus."

Lydia became Paul's first known convert in Europe and the first person to receive Christ in Philippi. The Bible says, "The Lord opened her heart to respond" to the message (Acts 16:14). The Lord began doing a good work in that city, and He began doing a good work in her life.

It wasn't a bad work; it was a good work. The moment the Lord opens your heart, He begins doing something good, something positive, in your life. He begins to change you from the inside out.

> **THE MOMENT THE LORD OPENS YOUR HEART, HE BEGINS DOING SOMETHING GOOD IN YOUR LIFE.**

Second, *God works inside us with all the energy of Christ.* In Colossians 1:29, Paul said, "I strenuously contend with all the energy Christ so powerfully works in me." We can too!

God's power isn't a triple-A battery. It's a billion kilowatts. He works powerfully with all the infinite energy of Christ. John Piper said, "God is always doing ten thousand things in your life, and you may be aware of only three of them."[1]

This is another way of talking about enthusiasm, which is a word from the Greek. The root word is *en* (within) plus *theos* (God). It means God within us—His energy working powerfully within us. Let me show you some more verses about serving God enthusiastically:

- Always work enthusiastically for the Lord, for you know that nothing you do for the Lord is ever useless. (1 Corinthians 15:58 NLT)
- Never be lazy, but work hard and serve the Lord enthusiastically. (Romans 12:11 NLT)
- Work with enthusiasm, as though you were working for the Lord rather than for people. (Ephesians 6:7 NLT)
- Whatever you do, do it enthusiastically, as something done for the Lord and not for men. (Colossians 3:23 HCSB)

This enthusiasm isn't something we work up. We're not talking about human zeal, but about the energy of God within us. It's what gives us strength, joy, perseverance, and effectiveness. How does He do this?

He Does It by His Holy Spirit

Third, *God works inside us through His Spirit.* Second Thessalonians 2:13 says, "God chose you . . . to be saved through the sanctifying work of the Spirit." The inner working of the Holy Spirit is what develops us step-by-step into carbon copies of the Lord Jesus Christ.

Second Corinthians 3:18 goes further to say we are "being transformed into his image" from one stage to another by that inner working of the Spirit of God.

Fourth, *God works inside us by His Word*. In 1 Thessalonians 2:13, Paul praised his readers for understanding the power of Scripture. "When you received the word of God, which you heard from us, you accepted it not as a human word, but as it actually is, the word of God, which is indeed at work in you who believe."

The other morning I awoke frustrated at myself. I was battling fatigue and wasn't keeping up with my disciplines as I should. *What is wrong?* I wondered. *Am I depressed? Am I old? What's wrong with me?*

I was using the New Living Translation in my Bible reading that morning, when I came to Psalm 29. Among other things, this psalm describes God's voice. "The voice of the LORD echoes above the sea" (v. 3). "The voice of the LORD is powerful; the voice of the LORD is majestic. The voice of the LORD splits the mighty cedar [trees]" (vv. 4–5). "The voice of the LORD strikes with bolts of lightning" (v. 7). "The voice of the LORD twists mighty oaks" (v. 9). Then the psalm ends with these words: "The LORD gives his people strength. The LORD blesses them with peace" (v. 11).

I prayed, "Lord, may Your voice echo through the canyons of my heart. May Your voice bounce from one side of my mind to the other. May Your voice echo throughout my life. May Your voice echo through my preaching and teaching and writing. May Your voice echo in the hearts of my children and grandchildren."

God accomplishes His work through the power of His voice, His Word. When we study His Word, His voice reverberates from one side of our soul to the other. Maybe you need to pray those same words today. The same voice that spoke the worlds into existence, that said, "Let there be light," that shouted, "It is finished," and the same voice that will shout the summons of resurrection at His return—*that voice* echoes throughout our lives and throughout our lifetimes, working in us what He desires. He gives His people strength and blesses them with peace.

GOD ACCOMPLISHES HIS WORK THROUGH THE POWER OF HIS VOICE, HIS WORD.

That's why we're devoted to being Bible students—daily readers of Scripture.

Fifth, *God works inside us as we ask Him to do so.* It helps if we make it a daily practice to specifically ask God to continue His work within us. As a pastor, I enjoyed praying the benediction over my congregation at the end of each service. Hebrews 13:20–21 was one of my favorite passages to use: "Now may the God of peace, who through the blood of the eternal covenant brought back from the dead our Lord Jesus, that great Shepherd of the sheep, equip you with everything good for doing his will, and may he work in us what is pleasing to him, through Jesus Christ, to whom be glory for ever and ever." May God equip every one of us to work His will.

Sixth, *God works inside us for His glory.* Why does God do all this? In Ephesians 3:20–21, Paul reminded the believers of God's purpose for working in us: "Now to him who is able to do immeasurably more than all we ask or imagine, according to his power that is at work within us, to him be glory in the church and in Christ Jesus throughout all generations, for ever and ever! Amen."

God wants to be glorified by His work within us, but He doesn't force it on us. Instead, He works inside us, giving us the desire and ability to fulfill His purpose. That brings us back to our primary text in Philippians 2: "Therefore, my dear friends, as you have always obeyed—not only in my presence, but now much more in my absence—continue to work out your salvation with fear and trembling, for it is God who works in you to will and to act according to His good purpose" (vv. 12–13).

Sometimes we want to do something but don't have the ability. Other times, we have the ability but not the desire. God works within us to give us both the desire and the ability to live for Him.

Here is a perfect prayer to pray when one or the other is missing in your life: "Lord, give me the desire and ability to serve You for Your glory."

Simply put

Work *Out* What God Is Working *In*

This, then, is the exciting life of the believer. Have you considered how personally this affects you? It's staggering. Almighty God, the Creator of the universe, *personally works within us!* He works within us from the day we respond to His gospel;

He works within us with all the energy of Christ; by the indwelling of the Holy Spirit; by the potency of His voice; in answer to prayer and for His glory; and He works within us to give us both the desire and the ability to do His good will.

But the command here is for us to *work out* what God is *working in* us. That's the outward life of faith and obedience. Charles Spurgeon said:

> We work out, bring out, educe from within ourselves to our exterior life, that which God constantly works in us in the interior secret recesses of our spiritual being. . . . You profess that the Holy Ghost dwells in you, and He does so if you are a Christian; well then, let your whole conduct be saturated with the sacred influence. . . . This is the matter to be attended to then, the bringing out, the working out, and developing the goldmine of grace which God has wrought in us.[2]

Author and Bible teacher Warren Wiersbe wrote, "Life is not a series of disappointing ups and downs. Rather it is a sequence of delightful ins and outs. God works in—we work out."[3]

I have found these prayers helpful:

> *"Lord, work on me, work in me, work through me, and work in spite of me today."*
>
> *"Lord, work on him, work in him, work through him, and work in spite of him today."*
>
> *"Lord, work on her, work in her, work through her, and work in spite of her today."*

We can pray, but only God can pry open the interior of someone's life to repair the wiring and renovate the heart.

> *Work in us by Thy gracious sway,*
> *And make Thy work appear,*
> *That all may feel and all may say,*
> *The Lord indeed is here.*[4]

Chapter 14

WHATEVER HAPPENS . . .

SHINE LIKE A STAR IN THE BLACKENED SKY

(PHILIPPIANS 2:14-18)

Heinrich Olbers, a German astronomer, lived in the early 1800s and is best known for his perplexing question, now known as Olbers' Paradox. "If the universe is filled with stars," he asked, "why is the sky dark at night?"

Olbers reasoned that if the universe is infinitely old and contains an infinite number of stars, then no matter where we look in space, our line of sight should end with a star. It's like being in the middle of a forest—everywhere we look, we see a tree. If the universe is filled with stars, then shouldn't the whole nighttime sky be filled with light? So why then is the nighttime sky black?[1]

One reason is that our universe is not infinite as earlier astronomists believed. It was created in a moment of time in the past, so the light from many stars hasn't yet reached earth.

But here's another reason that comes from the heart of God. I believe He put the burning stars into a dark sky to teach us something about our own lives and mission. He wants us to burn holes in the darkness. And that brings us to Philippians 2:14–16:

> Do everything without grumbling or arguing, so that you may become blameless and pure, "children of God without fault in a warped and crooked generation." Then you will shine among them like stars in the sky as you hold firmly to the word of life. And then I will be able to boast on the day of Christ that I did not run or labor in vain.

There's something extraordinary about this passage. According to Dr. Gordon Fee, this paragraph has a striking feature: "the sudden and profuse influx of echoes from the Old Testament, which is quite unlike anything else in the Pauline corpus. So unique is this that one scarcely knows what to make of it."[2]

Virtually every phrase of this passage comes from the Old Testament. It traces the story of the Old Testament Israelites. I'll show you how this works out.

Don't Grumble or Argue

First, we're to do everything without grumbling or complaining. In this passage, Paul harkened back to the Israelites, whose whole attitude was grumbling, murmuring, and complaining.

Exodus 15 records the exuberance that swept over the Israelites after God delivered them through the Red Sea and destroyed their enemies. They sang with euphoria. But in the next paragraph, they realized they had no drinkable water. "So the people grumbled against Moses, saying, 'What are we to drink?'" (Exodus 15:24).

The apostle Paul said, "Do not be like them."

I was a pastor for forty-three years, and like any pastor I had a few unhappy members. Over time I discovered something: If they were unhappy about one thing, they were likely right about that issue. But if they were unhappy about everything, they were probably wrong. All their judgments were influenced by an angry and complaining mood.

The Bible says, "To the pure, all things are pure" (Titus 1:15). In the same way, to those who are faultfinders, all things are faulty.

Orison Swett Marden said, "Everybody we meet is helped or hindered by what we radiate. It makes all the difference in the world whether we go about with a smiling face or wearing a frown. A smile in the heart not only changes the expression but it changes the whole nature which, as we know, takes on the color of our moods."[3] He also said, "No one can really be happy or successful unless he is master of his moods."[4]

This isn't easy. Recently someone treated me badly. I studied this passage in Philippians, and it spoke to my heart. But that very night I had a dream in which I told this man what I thought. I tore into him. The next morning, I put on my musical list of favorite hymns as I stepped into the shower, and the first song that came up was based on this broader passage in Philippians 2. The hymn spoke to my heart. "May the mind of Christ, my Savior, live in me from day to day; by His power and love controlling all I do and say."[5]

I said, "Lord, my consciousness is willing to forgive, but my subconsciousness is not."

I went back to Philippians 2 and studied it some more. Here's what I realized: I cannot grow spiritually without keeping a positive attitude about life. The unfolding logic of this passage says this plainly. We cannot grow spiritually unless we keep a biblically bright view of life.

> I CANNOT GROW SPIRITUALLY WITHOUT KEEPING A POSITIVE ATTITUDE ABOUT LIFE.

That's humility. Tim Keller said, "If you meet a truly humble person, you wouldn't think him or her humble, but happy and incredibly interested in you."[6]

Be Blameless and Pure

Why should we "do everything without grumbling or arguing"? The passage goes on to say, "so that you may become blameless and pure." There's something about a humble spirit of brightness that helps us become blameless.

When I was a boy, I went through a growth spurt. My mother had bought clothes for me that were one or two sizes too large. She said I would grow into them. She was right—they were too big, and then almost overnight, they fit perfectly, and then they began getting too tight.

We're clothed with the righteousness of Christ, but we have to grow into our spiritual duds. Our growth can be hindered by an unhappy and negative attitude. Here, again, we go back to the Israelites. In Deuteronomy 18:13–15, Moses said, "You must be blameless before the LORD your God. The nations you will dispossess listen to those who practice sorcery or divination. But as for you, the LORD your God has not permitted you to do so. The LORD your God will raise up for you a prophet like me from among you. . . . You must listen to him."

In the early days of photography, a rather sour and unpleasant woman went to have her picture made. She sat before the camera with a stern look on her face. The photographer pulled his head from under the black cloth and said, "Brighten up your eyes a little." She tried, but without success.

"Relax and let your face get into a cheerful mood."

"Look here," said the woman. "If you think an old woman can brighten up and an old face can soften up, you don't know anything about living."

"Oh yes, I do," said the photographer. "You have to work on it from the inside. It comes from the inside out. Now, try to get into a good mood and be cheerful and smile and let it show on your face."

Just as she did so, he snapped the picture.

When the picture arrived, her friends gathered around and said, "Oh, Catherine, you look so young and cheerful."

That evening she went into the bathroom and looked in the mirror. "If I could do that for the photographer," she said, "I can do it again." Every morning and evening, she stood in front of the mirror and said, "Brighten up your eyes a little. Relax and get your face into a cheerful mood. Work at it from the inside."

In this way, she became a younger, brighter, happier person.[7]

We have a divine photographer who has come out from under the dark shroud of death to say to us: *Rejoice in the Lord . . . This is the day I have made; rejoice and be glad in it . . . Be of good cheer; I have overcome the world . . . Do not fear . . . Be of good cheer.*

As we shake off our hurt feelings and negativism and listen to His Word, our hearts become younger, brighter, happier—and we grow into the righteousness of Christ.

Where does this happen? Right here, in the middle of a warped and crooked generation.

Realize You're in a Warped and Crooked World

Why be cheerful? Philippians 2:15 goes on to say, "so that you may become blameless and pure, 'children of God without fault in a warped and crooked generation.'" This is a quotation from Deuteronomy 32:5: "They are corrupt and not his children; to their shame they are a warped and crooked generation."

We need no convincing. As I was writing this, I read about how Andrew Thorburn lost his job. Thorburn was appointed chief executive of Essendon Football Club in Australia, but just thirty hours later, he was forced to resign because it turned out he is a Christian and a member of a Melbourne church that teaches biblical truth about gender, marriage, and sexuality. The football association said Thorburn's beliefs did not align "with values as a safe, inclusive, diverse, and welcoming club." Thorburn said plainly, "My personal Christian faith is not tolerated or permitted in the public square."[8]

Here in America, we've sunk to a level hard to imagine. I recently read a popular elementary school textbook on sexuality. I felt sick to my stomach from both the words and drawings I saw. All I can say is that if you have children in school, you need to know exactly what's in their textbooks. These are the same schools where the Bible is unwelcome and unwanted.

We're children of God in a warped and wicked age. But the Lord has us here for a purpose.

To Shine as Stars in the Sky, Holding Forth the Word of Life

Verse 15 continues, "Then you will shine among them like stars in the sky." This is also from the Old Testament. In Daniel 12:3, the Lord promised that "those who are wise will shine like the brightness of the heavens, and those who lead many to righteousness, like the stars for ever and ever."

Recently at a banquet, I was seated by a member of the Gideons International. This man lives in California and told me he frequently goes to UC Berkeley to give Bibles to students. He literally holds forth the Word of Life. I asked him if he received any opposition. "Yes, a lot," he said. One student came up him and belligerently asked, "Don't you have anything better to do with your time?"

"No," my friend replied. "I cannot think of one single thing that would be a better use of my time than giving free copies of the Bible to university students."

That young man cursed him and walked away, but there were other students who gladly received the Scriptures.

God put the burning stars into a dark sky to teach us something about our own lives and about the mission He has for us. We are to shine His light into a dark world. I cannot think of a single better way of using my time than by holding forth the Word of Life.

Then I Will Know I Did Not Labor in Vain

Paul ended the passage with a personal note. "And then I will be able to boast on the day of Christ that I did not run or labor in vain. But even if I am being poured out like a drink offering on the sacrifice and service coming from your faith, I am glad and rejoice with all of you. So you too should be glad and rejoice with me" (Philippians 2:16–18).

This portion reflects the drink offerings of Leviticus and also alludes to Isaiah 65:23, which promises we will not labor in vain because we will be blessed by the Lord.

Earlier this year Jeff and Heather Brigstock invited me to a book signing at their coffee shop at South Water Manor in Gallatin, Tennessee. When I arrived, they said, "This is here because of you."

Seeing my perplexity, Jeff reminded me of a time some years before when I'd been speaking in Ireland. His parents were there, seated at the same table

I was, and told me they had a son in Nashville who was so discouraged he thought God no longer wanted to use him. Apparently I gave the couple my phone number, and told them to have their son call me after I returned home. Some months later, Jeff called me, and we met for coffee.

I have little recollection of our meeting, but Jeff told me how our conversation that day changed his life, his direction, his perception of himself and ministry, and eventually led to him and Heather opening South Water Manor in Gallatin, which is a beehive of ministry in that community.[9]

I was encouraged to realize that the Lord has used me in ways I can't even remember. The same is true for you. We're doing greater good than we know, and our labor in the Lord is not in vain.

Let this divine passage come true in you. Do everything without grumbling or arguing so that you can be blameless and pure, a child of God without fault in a warped and crooked generation, where you shine like a star in the sky as you hold forth the Word of Life.

Let's keep on shining and sharing, trusting the Lord to bless our efforts in ways we may not realize until we get to heaven.

Chapter 15

WHATEVER HAPPENS . . .

STAY AS CHEERFUL AS POSSIBLE IN ALL CIRCUMSTANCES

(PHILIPPIANS 2:19-24)

While in Switzerland a few years ago, I was delighted to see the cattle grazing in the pastures among the Alps. They wore bells around their necks, and you could hear them chiming and jingling like so many church carillons. I loved the sound.

I thought the cows wore bells so if any wandered away, they could be easily found. That's partially true, but I've since learned about the science that goes into cowbells. They're tuned to different notes and different octaves, all designed to create an ambiance that has a therapeutic and cheerful influence on the cows, causing them to be more productive and give better milk. The peals also lift the spirits of the farmers and residents of the valley. There is always music in the air.

There's a lesson in that. Even when we're in the valley, there should be something cheerful going on in our

> EVEN WHEN WE'RE IN THE VALLEY, THERE SHOULD BE SOMETHING CHEERFUL GOING ON IN OUR HEARTS.

hearts. If we listen closely, we can hear the same notes in Paul's paragraph about Timothy in Philippians 2:19–24:

> I hope in the Lord Jesus to send Timothy to you soon, that I also may be cheered when I receive news about you. I have no one else like him, who will show genuine concern for your welfare. For everyone looks out for their own interests, not those of Jesus Christ. But you know that Timothy has proved himself, because as a son with his father he has served with me in the work of the gospel. I hope, therefore, to send him as soon as I see how things go with me. And I am confident in the Lord that I myself will come soon.

You'll remember that, just as the apostle Paul was ready to launch his fourth missionary tour, he was arrested and spent five or so precious years in various conditions of imprisonment. At the time he wrote this letter to the Philippians, he was either still detained in his own rented house in Rome or he had been moved to a holding cell closer to the imperial tribunal. He knew the case against him was weak, and he also had a powerful weapon—his official Roman citizenship. He expected to be released, but he wasn't certain. So he told the Philippians he would send Timothy with news as soon as he knew how things would go.

We don't know how old Timothy was when Paul unofficially adopted him and began taking him with him on his travels, but most think that at this point, he was perhaps in his twenties. Notice how Paul described him: "As a son with his father he has served with me in the work of the gospel."

Paul was using Timothy as an example of what he had been discussing in his letter. He had told the Philippians to look not to their own interests but to those of Jesus Christ and to have a genuine concern for others. Now he was showing them a living, breathing, true-life example of that instruction.

"You need to be like Jesus and have the mind of Christ," Paul was saying. "It's not impossible—look at Timothy and you'll see a Christlike man, someone whose example you can follow."

In context, that's what this paragraph is about. But there's something more here too. As I've read this paragraph over and over, three phrases have stood out to me.

Be Concerned but Not Anxious

The first phrase is built around the word *concern*: "I have no one else like him, who will show genuine concern for your welfare."

Here's what's so interesting to me: The Greek word for concern is *merimnao*, which is the same word we find later in Philippians 4:6: "Do not be *anxious* about anything."

In chapter 2, Paul commended Timothy for being *merimnao*, but in chapter 4 he told us not to be *merimnao*. Of course, even in English, the word "concern" has a range of meanings, depending on the context:

She's going to tell a story *concerning* her mother.

She's always *concerned* about the needs of her community.

She's very *concerned* because her daughter is in danger.

So how do the two situations above work together? The psychological balance between Philippians 2 and Philippians 4 is a supernatural one. As we go through life, it's good to be concerned, but it isn't good to be anxious. Be concerned for others but be anxious for nothing.

In my book *Worry Less, Live More*, I wrote: "I've often wondered how to know, at any given time, if I'm reasonably concerned or unreasonably alarmed. It's a difficult median, but here's the key: When our concern is healthy, it doesn't debilitate us. When it begins to feel debilitating, it has morphed into worry, which becomes a vicious cycle."[1]

That's very hard for me, but let's keep digging into this paragraph because there's another phrase that brings even more balance—*that I may be cheered.*

Be Cheerful but Not Naive

Again in verses 19 and 20, Paul said, "I hope in the Lord Jesus to send Timothy to you soon, that I also may be cheered when I receive news about you. I have no one else like him, who will show genuine concern for your welfare."

The balance for psychological well-being is to be concerned but not anxious, and cheerful but not naive. This is a helpful reminder to me because I've always struggled with these things. I think I was born in the negative case. Once when I was in college, I was moping around, depressed and discouraged. Sometimes I had trouble getting out of bed because of despondency.

One day my roommate, Bill, came into the room and said, "Robert, I've been studying the life of the great evangelist Dwight L. Moody, and you remind me of him."

"How is that?" I said.

"Because you're moody."

If you're moody, I want to encourage you to do what I've done. Go through the Bible and find out what it says about the joyful life. Using the word search function at Bible Gateway in the New International Version, I was surprised to find how many times the following "joyful words" appear in Scripture:

- The word "joy" occurs 242, either in the verses or in the headings.
- The word "rejoice" occurs 177 times.
- The word "blessed" occurs 217 times.
- The word "glad" occurs 108 times.
- The word "delight" occurs 105 times.
- The word "comfort" occurs 71 times.
- The word "celebrate" occurs 68 times.
- The word "enjoy" occurs 57 times.
- The word "happy" occurs 20 times.
- This word "cheer" occurs 13 times.
- The word "merry" occurs 5 times.
- And so does the word "overjoyed"—5 times.

That's 1,088 times the Bible talks about being cheerful. It comes almost exactly to three verses for every day of the year, without repeating any of them. I can tell you from personal experience that nothing compares to searching out these verses and making a list of the ones that the Lord especially wants to give you. Write them down. Put them on cards. Memorize them. Internalize them.

When you feel anxious, go to your cheerful verses and claim them. Find ways of keeping these verses at the forefront of your attention.

WHEN YOU FEEL ANXIOUS, GO TO YOUR CHEERFUL VERSES AND CLAIM THEM.

Julie Chapman, an elementary school teacher at Chattahoochee Elementary School north of Atlanta, was diagnosed with cancer. She struggled bitterly with it, but her students and friends sent her many messages, often with Bible verses included. Every time Julie received a Bible verse from someone, she wrote it on a sticky note and posted it on her wall. Her walls were covered with verses. She literally surrounded herself with Scripture. Eventually she compiled them all on the walls of her bathroom, and I've seen a picture of that room in an article in her local newspaper. The headline said: "For Julie Chapman, Beating Cancer Came Down to Faith, Family, and Sticky Notes."[2]

Krystal Whitten is a wife and mother in Tampa who, when she was in high school, loved to write out Bible verses in a creative style with Crayola markers. She posted them on the wall of her bedroom. In college, she studied graphic design. But as an adult and a wife, she got away from the Bible. Her mother became ill and then passed away, and Krystal went through some dark times. For years, she had no interest in reading the Bible.

One day a friend invited her to a Bible study that provided free childcare. The study group would read a book of the Bible each week, then gather to discuss it. Soon Krystal found herself reading the Bible every day and becoming reacquainted with it. It came alive to her, and one day she selected a verse and wrote it out in a creative style using hand lettering. In the process, she found she had memorized the verse. She framed it and put it on the wall, and every time she went by it she said it in her mind.[3]

Now Krystal has a bestselling resource entitled *Lettering Prayer Journal*. Her work is on gift cards, tea towels, and framed prints. She wants to help people surround themselves with Bible verses.

I love these ideas, for God wants us to be concerned without being anxious and cheerful without being naive. But beneath it all is one powerful truth— and that's the third phrase I want to give you.

Be in the Lord Jesus

Notice how Paul begins and ends this paragraph: "I hope in the Lord Jesus to send Timothy to you soon . . . I am confident in the Lord that I myself will come soon." *In the Lord.* The phrase means something to Paul. Look at these verses too:

- "And because of my chains, most of the brothers and sisters have become confident *in the Lord* and dare all the more to proclaim the gospel without fear." (Philippians 1:14)
- "So then, welcome him *in the Lord* with great joy." (Philippians 2:29)
- "Further, my brothers and sisters, rejoice *in the Lord.*" (Philippians 3:1)
- "Therefore, my brothers and sisters, you whom I love and long for, my joy and crown, stand firm *in the Lord.*" (Philippians 4:1)

This phrase occurs nine times in the book of Philippians, and the related phrase "in Christ" occurs another eight times. This is Paul's signature phrase. If you could take all thirteen of Paul's epistles, squeeze them all together and reduce them to one phrase, this would be it. "In Christ." This phrase occurs over two hundred times in his writings.[4]

Scholars have a hard time pinning down all that Paul meant to convey with this phrase. What does it mean?

It means you are no longer outside. You're an insider. You are inside the love and redemption of Jesus Christ. You are in union with Him. The Gospel of John calls this "abiding in Christ." Your whole life is lived within His grace.

The summer after I graduated from college, I was part of a gospel team that toured the Northeast. In one camp, I served a group of middle-school boys, and I thought I'd take them camping one night. We hiked about an hour through the woods to a clearing. We built a campfire and talked about the Lord Jesus, then everyone fell asleep under the stars. About 2:00 a.m., I was jolted awake by water thrown in my face. At first, I thought one of those boys was playing a trick, but I quickly realized the rain was

YOU'RE AN INSIDER. YOU ARE INSIDE THE LOVE AND REDEMPTION OF JESUS CHRIST.

coming down in torrents. The boys all jumped out of their sleeping bags, and we gathered everything up. There was no shelter anywhere. We had to hike back an hour in the cold, driving rain.

Imagine how good it felt to get into that dry cabin, into a hot shower, into a warm bed.

Today so many people are standing out in the cold rain, outside of Christ, outside of peace, outside of the eternal life He gives. Jesus said in John 10:9, "I am the door. If anyone enters by Me, he will be saved" (NKJV).

When you are in the Lord Jesus Christ, He provides the foundation for staying as cheerful as possible. He helps you to grow emotionally and spiritually, to become someone who knows how to be concerned without anxiety and how to be cheerful without being naive.

Whatever happens, let's live like that.

Chapter 16

WHATEVER HAPPENS . . .

NEVER THINK OF QUITTING

(PHILIPPIANS 2:25-30)

Chris Edmonds, a Tennessee pastor, became curious to know about his father's military service during World War II. It took some detective work, but finally Pastor Edmonds learned of his father's heroism.

Sergeant Roddie Edmonds from Knoxville, Tennessee, had fought in the Battle of the Bulge. He was captured and sent to a POW camp where he was the highest-ranking GI and in charge of all the POWs there. There were over a thousand American soldiers at the camp, and some were Jewish. One day the Nazi commandant demanded that Sergeant Edmonds identify the American Jews. Under Edmonds's command, all 1,292 soldiers stepped forward. When the German officer saw the group, he turned to Edmonds in anger and said he only wanted the Jews. Edmonds replied, "We are all Jews here."

The commandant threatened to shoot the sergeant, but Edmonds told him he would have to kill all the men because they would report him for war crimes after the Allies won.

Later Edmonds realized that some of the POWs were on the verge of giving up. He divided the soldiers into two groups, those who were up and those who were down, as he put it. He assigned one "up" man to one "down" man, and this way kept the soldiers alive.

After the war, he returned home and told nobody about what had happened. He made his quiet living as a salesman and sang in churches.[1]

Edmonds was a man who never thought of quitting. We have heroes like that in the Bible, too, and some of them are minor characters, like Epaphroditus, whom Paul referred to in military terms as a soldier.

> But I think it is necessary to send back to you Epaphroditus, my brother, co-worker and fellow soldier, who is also your messenger, whom you sent to take care of my needs. For he longs for all of you and is distressed because you heard he was ill. Indeed he was ill, and almost died. But God had mercy on him, and not on him only but also on me, to spare me sorrow upon sorrow. Therefore I am all the more eager to send him, so that when you see him again you may be glad and I may have less anxiety. So then, welcome him in the Lord with great joy, and honor people like him, because he almost died for the work of Christ. He risked his life to make up for the help you yourselves could not give me. (Philippians 2:25–30)

The backstory is important here, and I've touched on it before. Paul, Silas, Timothy, and Luke showed up in the vast Roman city of Philippi and planted a church. In the process, Paul and Silas were arrested and flogged. Afterward the Philippian church felt very close to Paul and sent him financial aid wherever he was. When they heard he was under house arrest in Rome, they took up another offering.

One of the members of the church, Epaphroditus, said, "I can travel to Rome and stay with Paul as long as needed. I'll take our offering and stay as his helper." The church commissioned him and he traveled more than eight hundred miles over land and sea until he found Paul in Rome.

It must have been a joyful reunion as Epaphroditus gave Paul all the news from Philippi. Epaphroditus then went to work, perhaps washing Paul's clothes, preparing his food, and greeting his guests. But he soon became deathly ill, and Paul tried to save his life.

When Epaphroditus recovered, Paul thought it best to send him home and have him take the Philippian letter with him. The apostle didn't want the Philippians to think Epaphroditus had failed in his mission, so he added this paragraph to the letter, describing his friend using five different terms.

Brother

First, he called Epaphroditus his brother: "But I think it is necessary to send back to you Epaphroditus, my brother." God designed His church as a gigantic family—the largest family on earth. We're not just an organization or an enterprise like other groups. Take Coca-Cola, for example. They have their product in every nation in the world.[2] The same secret formula is used. Yet the seven hundred thousand global employees are not brothers and sisters.

When we come to Christ, we're born into His kingdom and adopted into His family. We call God our Father. It's not *like* a family; it *is* a family. Some time ago, I was in Myanmar where I met Christians from all over the Asia/Pacific realm. The moment I met them, I loved them and felt a kinship with them I can't explain.

> GOD DESIGNED HIS CHURCH AS A GIGANTIC FAMILY— THE LARGEST FAMILY ON EARTH.

I recall hearing a story years ago of an American army officer on an island in the South Pacific. Every Sunday he left the base to attend church in the nearby village. Someone asked him why he did it. He said, "Well, on the base they call me Lieutenant. On the island they call me GI Joe. But in the church, they call me brother."

Coworker

Second, Paul called him his coworker: "But I think it is necessary to send back to you Epaphroditus, my . . . co-worker."

We almost never see the apostle Paul working alone. He was left alone in Athens, and that didn't go well. By the time he got to Corinth, he was in bad shape. From the very beginning when he set off with Barnabas, he always recruited coworkers. In his writings, Paul used the words "fellow worker" or "co-worker" to describe fifteen different people or groups. They include Timothy, Apollos, Silas, Titus, Priscilla, Aquila, Urban, Philemon, Mark, Aristarchus, Demas, Luke, Justus, Epaphroditus, and the entire Corinthian church.[3]

The prophet Elijah tried to work alone, but when he broke down under the strain, God gave him Elisha. In a similar way, Jesus sent out His disciples two by two. Even Jesus Christ, Son of Man and Son of God, wanted His disciples near Him. He needed their fellowship.

One drop of water is a beautiful thing—it has shape and clarity. But I'd never put just one drop on a plant. I have a potted Japanese maple on my patio, and when I water it, I may pour a gallon of water into the soil. There are 90,921 drops of water in a gallon. It takes all of us working together to keep this world alive and hydrated with the waters of the Holy Spirit.

Fellow Soldier

Paul also called Epaphroditus his fellow soldier. Paul was writing this while under Roman imprisonment. He may have still been under house arrest, but in those days they didn't have ankle monitors. They had soldiers, and Paul was chained to one all the time. He drew a lot of literary inspiration from that.

In Ephesians 6:10–18, he described the soldier's armor and suggested each piece as symbolic for the armor of the believer. In 2 Timothy 2:3, he encouraged Timothy to be a good soldier of Jesus Christ. I've never been in the military, and I've always felt conflicted about that. The stories about the men and women in our armed forces grip me. Being a soldier is not for the faint of heart.

I was reading about the marines in the Korean War one day when I was low in spirits and feeling sorry for myself. My transition from the church I loved had been distressing, and I told someone at the grocery store I felt like a man without a country. I was brooding over that when I came back home and resumed my story of the Korean War—and I felt ashamed as I read about all they went through.

In his book *Ship of Miracles*, Bert Gilbert quoted an army report about the American troops in Korea:

> They were only a few weeks away from the scenes of home, but it seemed like a thousand years. Then most of them had been recruits. Now they were veterans. They had fought their fight and knew they would fight again; but it wouldn't be something strange and unknown next time. Now, there were heroes among them and others who no longer answered roll call.[4]

The Bible says we must "endure hardship as a good soldier of Jesus Christ" (2 Timothy 2:3 NKJV). It would be good for us to more frequently think of ourselves as soldiers in the army of the Lord.

Messenger

There's a fourth word Paul used to describe Epaphroditus—he was a messenger: "But I think it is necessary to send back to you Epaphroditus . . . who is also your messenger, whom you sent to take care of my needs."

The word "messenger" here is the Greek word *apostolos*, from which we get *apostle*—one who is sent. Epaphroditus volunteered to be sent on a short-term mission trip to care for Paul's needs. The entire congregation could not go. Perhaps they wanted to, but most of them had families and jobs or physical or financial limitations. But one man was able to go. He volunteered, and he was sent as an apostle for the rest.

What was his message? It must have been one of encouragement. He was an apostle of encouragement. "Now when you get to Rome and track down Paul, you encourage him," the Philippians might have said. "Let him know we love him and we're praying for him. Tell him we'll continue sending him money for his needs. And give him some Scripture."

We need to be apostles of encouragement.

Remember earlier how Sergeant Roddie Edmonds realized that some of the POWs were on the verge of giving up, so he

WE NEED TO BE APOSTLES OF ENCOURAGEMENT.

assigned one "up" man to each "down" man, to encourage them and keep those soldiers alive? Let's be *up* people, apostles of encouragement.

Caregiver

Finally, Paul referred to Epaphroditus as a caregiver (minister): "But I think it is necessary to send back to you Epaphroditus . . . whom you sent to take care of my needs."

The word "care" here, used as *to take care of,* is a noun in the Greek and it really means caregiver. The New American Standard Bible states verse 25 in a way that helps us clearly see the five roles Paul referenced: "But I thought it necessary to send to you Epaphroditus, my brother and fellow worker and fellow soldier, who is also your messenger and minister to my need."

It's interesting to note that Epaphroditus was sent to Rome to be Paul's caregiver, but in a twist of events, Paul became his caregiver.

My wife, Katrina, had multiple sclerosis for twenty-five years before she passed away. The last few years were hard, but often when someone referred to me as her caregiver, I'd correct them. I'd tell them we were each other's caregivers. I did some things for her, yes. But she was the strength and stability of my life.

We never know when one or another of us will become sick or maybe even be imprisoned for the gospel. But it doesn't matter—our calling is to be caregivers for one another.

Honor Where Honor Is Due

Let's conclude this study with verses 29 and 30: "So then, welcome [Epaphroditus] in the Lord with great joy, and honor people like him, because he almost died for the work of Christ. He risked his life to make up for the help you yourselves could not give me."

Names meant a lot in Bible times, and this man was named Epaphroditus.

His name literally meant "honored by Aphrodite." She was the Greek goddess of love and sex. His parents were apparently pagans who worshipped the goddess of love and sex. They had devoted their son's life to the honor of Aphrodite.

But somewhere, somehow, Epaphroditus had come to faith in Jesus Christ. Now he was a brother, a fellow worker for Christ, a soldier of the cross, an ambassador of encouragement, and a caregiver. Instead of being honored by Aphrodite, now he would be honored by the Philippians.

The Bible says to give honor to whom honor is due (Romans 13:7). When you find someone who is a living demonstration of the kind of life Paul described in Philippians 2—someone who is Christlike and Timothy-like and Epaphroditus-like, someone who is a brother or sister, a fellow worker, a soldier of the cross, an ambassador of encouragement, and a caregiver for others— honor that person. Their lives are valuable, and they are not afraid to risk them for the cause of Christ.

New Testament believers like Epaphroditus faced daunting circumstances, endured great hardships, and lived in a pagan culture as bad or worse than ours. But they never quit. They were brothers and sisters, fellow workers, soldiers, ambassadors, and ready to care for others whatever the cost.

Whatever happens, let's be like them.

Whatever happens, don't think of quitting.

Chapter 17

WHATEVER HAPPENS . . .

LEARN THE TECHNIQUES OF SPIRITUAL SELF-DEFENSE

(PHILIPPIANS 3:1-3)

Everyone's trying to figure out why the world is so violent. There might be legislative reasons or laws that need to be changed, but at the heart of it is one simple thing—when a society turns away from the truth of Scripture, it begins to disintegrate.

According to the book of Genesis, in the days before the flood, "the earth was corrupt in God's sight and was full of violence" (Genesis 6:11). Jesus said, "As it was in the days of Noah, so it will be at the coming of the Son of Man" (Matthew 24:37). He said that the last days would be characterized by "the increase of wickedness" (Matthew 24:12).

Second Timothy 3:1–3 says, "There will be terrible times in the last days. People will be lovers of themselves . . . boastful, proud, abusive . . . without love . . . without self-control, brutal."

How are we to stay safe in a world like this?

I cannot guarantee we will never experience threats, danger, acts of violence, thefts, or any of the rest of it. All over the world, violence is being directed against the people of God. We're living in a dangerous world, and that's all there is to it.

But we can live so that Satan will never be able to truly hurt us in any ultimate way. Paul gives us five techniques for spiritual self-defense in Philippians 3:1–3:

> Brothers and sisters, rejoice in the Lord! It is no trouble for me to write the same things to you again, and it is a safeguard for you. Watch out for those dogs, those evildoers, those mutilators of the flesh. For it is we who are the circumcision, we who serve God by his Spirit, who boast in Christ Jesus, and who put no confidence in the flesh.

As I've pointed out, Paul's great theme in Philippians is, "Whatever happens, conduct yourselves in a manner worthy of Jesus Christ, standing firm in the faith in one spirit." So far he has illustrated how Jesus, Timothy, and Epaphroditus did that. In chapter three, he showed us how he himself was doing that, and by the end of the passage, recommended they follow his example. In fact, as we'll see later, he told them no less than three times to follow his example.

But a new element is introduced here—that of setting needed safeguards into place in the church and in our lives.

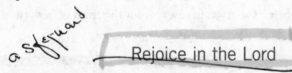

Rejoice in the Lord

The first thing he told them here was to rejoice in the Lord: "Further, my brothers and sisters, rejoice in the Lord! It is no trouble for me to write the same things to you again, and it is a safeguard for you" (3:1). This isn't a suggestion. It's a commandment to rejoice in the Lord. This attitude, this activity, this habit will be a safeguard to them.

The Greek word for safeguard, *asphales*, means to be secure and rendered safe. In other words, we rejoice in the Lord because that attitude is like a protective shield around us.

I have never thought of joy like this before. I've studied this subject in the Bible for years. I've looked up every verse I could find about joy and rejoicing and gladness and cheer, as I recommended for you in an earlier chapter. I've written about it, preached about it, and learned something about the power of a joyful life. I've known and memorized many verses about joy.

> **WE REJOICE IN THE LORD BECAUSE THAT ATTITUDE IS LIKE A PROTECTIVE SHIELD AROUND US.**

safeguard

I recall the first time I really got hold of Nehemiah 8:10: "The joy of the LORD is your strength." I've visualized joy as an energy factory inside of me, generating enthusiasm and strength for living.

I recall finding Psalm 100 at a time when I was serving the Lord out of a sense of duty and drudgery. It says, "Make a joyful noise unto the LORD, all ye lands. Serve the LORD with gladness" (vv. 1–2 KJV). That really changed the way I went into every day's duties.

When I read about the fruit of the Spirit in Galatians 5:22–23, I realized that I could not, within my own natural self, produce the joy of the Lord. I had to be yielded and open to the Spirit so that He could produce it for me and in me and through me.

I also learned the importance of joy in leadership during a difficult time in my pastoral career. It seemed like everything had gone wrong at the same time in serious ways. I was overwhelmed and on the verge of faltering under it all. But the Lord gave me fifteen Bible verses about joy and told me to go onto the platform and smile and teach the Bible with joy. Something about that reassured the people, steadied the church, and got us to a better place.

So I've thought of joy as an electrical generator, as the necessary ingredient for Christian service, as a result of the Holy Spirit's working in my life, and as a powerful mechanism for leadership. But I had never before thought of joy as a safeguard, as a shield, as a weapon, as an invisible cloak around me, or as a guardian who served as a security officer.

When I go to churches as a guest speaker, I'm usually met and shadowed by one or more security officers. At one church, some of them are off-duty Navy SEALs. I love those guys and I'm never afraid of anything when they're nearby. But I had never thought of joy as a Navy SEAL assigned to me by God for my own security. But here's Philippians 3:1, informing us that the joy of the Lord is the safeguard of our souls.

Paul drew from the book of Psalms here, I'm sure. The psalms tell us over and over to rejoice in the Lord. I have a whole list of references, but I don't think it's necessary to give them. Paul was using the language of David. What does it mean to rejoice in the Lord? It means you have developed the habit of elevating your innermost spirit by learning to recall all the truth you know about the Lord and His grace toward you. Do you need some reminders of those truths? Here are just a few:

There is a God, and He made you.

He knows your name.

He knows your failures, but He still loves you.

He knows your weakness but helps you.

He knows your problems but guides you through them.

Jesus came and died for you.

He rose again.

He ascended to heaven.

He reigns in authority.

He is coming in glory.

He has given us the Bible with all we need to know within its covers.

He wants to use us and has a plan for our lives.

The troubles of this world are passing away.

The day of His return is drawing near.

We are heirs of God and coheirs with Christ.

Heaven is ahead of us.

And we are "persuaded that neither death nor life, nor angels nor principalities nor powers, nor things present nor things to come, nor height nor depth, nor any other created thing, shall be able to separate us from the love of God which is in Christ Jesus our Lord" (Romans 8:38–39 NKJV).

You cannot bring those things to mind again and again without your heart and spirit being elevated. There is joy in the Lord. And there is joy in all there is about the Lord.

The joy of the Lord is a safeguard. It protects you against fear and paranoia, dejection and despondency, weariness and worry, temptation and sin, pain and sorrow, and the devil and his demonic forces.

Satan doesn't know what to do with a joyful Christian. He can do a lot with believers who have lost their joy, but you might as well try to hold an inflated basketball underwater as try to submerge a joy-inflated Christian. Joy is an attitude, an activity, and a piece of armor. It is a safeguard for the soul.

Watch Out for Error

The second way to safeguard ourselves is by watching out for errors and adhering to the truth of Scripture. Verse 2 says: "Watch out for those dogs, those evildoers, those mutilators of the flesh."

Paul referred to false teachers here as dogs. Now, most of us love dogs. I don't have a dog because I travel too much and don't want to take care of one, but people love their dogs. It wasn't that way in biblical times. Dogs were scavengers, running wild, and the Jews considered them unclean. So Paul used that word to characterize the false teachers who were dogging him everywhere.

Who were they? They were Judaizers—teachers who believed you had to convert to Judaism or at least adopt Jewish practices if you wanted to become a Christian. They said a person had to receive Christ as Savior—*plus* be circumcised, *plus* keep the Jewish calendar, *plus* keep the Jewish diet, and so on if they wanted to be saved. Jesus was a Jew, they said, and Christianity was the evolution of Judaism, so anyone who wanted to embrace Christianity had to embrace Judaism. But it wasn't true.

After the Messiah was born, He established the church. Under His instruction, the church was made up of both Jews and Gentiles. To some Jewish believers, the ritual of circumcision was so important they thought a Gentile man could not be saved without undergoing this medical procedure.

They would say, "Oh, good. You want to become a Christian? Let's go see a surgeon."

As you can imagine, that was a significant barrier to church growth. Plus it was totally unnecessary and untrue.

Paul spent vast portions of his ministry fighting this heresy. Just read Galatians 5. His message was that we are saved by grace through faith alone. We do not have to come to Christ through Judaism. We come to Him just as we are, by faith alone. It's not faith *plus* ritual, or faith *plus* circumcision, or faith *plus* baptism—or faith *plus* anything.

To keep yourself safe, Paul told the Philippians, you need to guard your theology and keep your beliefs anchored to Scripture.

I don't know of anyone today preaching the exact same Judaizing message that Paul confronted, but the danger of false teachers is greater now than ever. If you're thinking of joining a church, make sure you know what they teach and believe.

When I was a pastor, we articulated our beliefs in our church's printed materials as well as on our website. We talked about the Bible, the person of God, the person of Christ, the nature of salvation, the Holy Spirit, the second coming.

In many churches, those articles of faith have been replaced by statements about human diversity, radical inclusion, social justice, tolerance, religious pluralism, affirmation, and reconciliation. One church website said, "We are inclusive. We have spiritual practices, not dogma."

Some of that sounds pretty good, but much of it is code language for beliefs that are distinctly unbiblical. And notice what's missing in many church statements: There is nothing about God, nothing about the Bible, nothing about sin or justification or redemption, nothing about eternal life and death, and nothing about heaven or hell. Jesus is often only referenced as a teacher who taught us to love others and minister to the marginalized.

Well, He did do that, but there's much more about Him, isn't there?

From the beginning of my ministry, I've believed that there cannot be biblical conduct without biblical content. Trendy sermons and motivational talks don't build a church or those who attend it. The pulpit is not a practice field but a battlefield. Our weapons are not sticky points but Bible verses, well exegeted in their context. My greatest joy as a pastor was teaching and preaching "to further the faith of God's elect and their knowledge of the truth that leads to godliness" (Titus 1:1). Other goals are laudatory, but this is mandatory. The pulpit is the foundation of a healthy church; the Word of God is the foundation of the pulpit; and Christ is the cornerstone.

THERE CANNOT BE BIBLICAL CONDUCT WITHOUT BIBLICAL CONTENT.

We cannot be safe if we don't rejoice in the Lord and maintain our biblical theology, doctrine, worldview, and lifestyle.

When Margaret Thatcher was prime minister of England, she kept an eye on Saddam Hussein's invasion of Kuwait in August 1990, and wasn't having it. She famously pulled George H. W. Bush aside at a diplomatic meeting and told him, "Remember, George, this is no time to go wobbly."

That's what I would say to the church in America today. That's what I would say to pastors and Christian schools at every level. It's what I would say to you: This is no time to go wobbly. Whatever happens, learn the techniques of spiritual self-defense—the joy of the Lord and the truthfulness of our Gospel.

Chapter 18

WHATEVER HAPPENS . . .

VALUE CHRIST OVER COMMAS

(PHILIPPIANS 3:4-7)

Abigail Disney, the grandniece of Walt Disney, was raised amid wealth and fame in North Hollywood. She now has some controversial things to say about rich people. Speaking at an event, she said a hallmark of billionaires is seeing whose plane is biggest. The more money her parents got, she said, the more they were afraid of interacting with others. They didn't know who to trust. People wanted them for their fame and fortune, not for their friendship. They had to have special entrances and exits everywhere, a private plane, a private bar.

At a certain point for rich people, Abigail said, life becomes all about the commas.[1] If you have a thousand dollars, you have one comma—1,000. If you have a million dollars, you have two commas—1,000,000. If you have a billion dollars, you have three commas—1,000,000,000. Now the world is waiting to see who the first trillionaire will be. He or she will have four commas.

For some people, life is simply an accumulation of commas—but commas can all be erased at any moment. Paul had some commas, too, but after meeting

Christ, he relegated them to a lower place in life. Christ, he knew, is better than all the commas in the world.

It's not the comma that makes for a fulfilling life. It's Christ. He wrote:

> If someone else thinks they have reasons to put confidence in the flesh, I have more: circumcised on the eighth day, of the people of Israel, of the tribe of Benjamin, a Hebrew of Hebrews; in regard to the law, a Pharisee; as for zeal, persecuting the church; as for righteousness based on the law, faultless. But whatever were gains to me I now consider loss for the sake of Christ. (Philippians 3:4–7)

As we saw in the last chapter, we're now in the section of Philippians where Paul warned his readers against Judaizers. Who were these people? The *Lexham Bible Dictionary* says:

> The English word *Judaizer* connotes the practicing of imposing Jewish religious and social customs on others. Some Christian Judaizers (e.g., many of Paul's opponents; the Jewish teachers of Acts 15:1) imposed the requirements of the Mosaic Law—primarily but not exclusively circumcision, Sabbath-keeping, and dietary laws—on Gentile Christians, insisting that salvation, or being a member of the people of God, rested on obedience to the Mosaic law.[2]

Jesus was creating a church that transcended Judaism. That was hard for the early Jewish believers to realize. It took time for even the apostles to understand what God was doing. The Lord had created a church, and the membership requirement was simply repentance and faith—not Jewish ritual. Some of the Jewish people who were drawn to Christ couldn't understand how Gentiles could bypass Jewish ritual and enter directly into the kingdom. So they were preaching that in order to follow Christ, one had to also embrace Jewish practices.

THE LORD HAD CREATED A CHURCH, AND THE MEMBERSHIP REQUIREMENT WAS SIMPLY REPENTANCE AND FAITH.

Not so, said Paul.

What Paul Said

If anyone on this earth could have been saved by keeping the external demands of the Jewish system and Mosaic law, it was Paul. And he was quick to say so. Here in verses four through seven, he listed seven elements of his Jewish resume. I've separated them with commas.

- Paul was circumcised on the eighth day (of his life as prescribed by the Law for male Jewish babies),
- Of the people of Israel,
- Of the tribe of Benjamin (the tribe of origin for Israel's first king for whom Paul, as Saul of Tarsus, was named),
- A Hebrew of Hebrews (he was of pure Jewish stock; his parents were fully Jewish with no other blood mingled in their lineage),
- In regard to the law, he was a Pharisee (a strict denomination among the Jews, one known for its conservative approach to the Old Testament),
- As for zeal, he had persecuted the church, and
- As for righteousness based on the law, he was faultless. (This doesn't mean Paul thought he was sinless, but he scrupulously kept the rules about Sabbath observance, dietary laws, and ritual cleanness.)

With all those credentials, if anyone could have been able to obtain salvation through Judaism, it was Paul.

This reminds me of Martin Luther. As a young man, he entered a monastery and tried to be so perfect as a monk that he could be saved by his good works. He said, "I was a good monk, and I kept the rules of my order so strictly that I may say that if ever a monk got to heaven by his monkery, it was I. All my brothers at the monastery who knew me would bear me out. If I had kept on any longer, I should have killed myself with vigils, prayers, reading, and other work."[3]

His life was saved when he learned we are saved by grace through faith.

You may ask what any of that has to do with life today, and I would say a great deal. There are many churches, denominations, branches, and varieties of Christianity in which people believe they can be right with God and have eternal life by keeping various rituals or living an outwardly good life.

The American Worldview Inventory 2020 Survey, conducted by the Cultural Research Center at Arizona Christian University, studied people who identified themselves as Christian. The researchers asked what religion they held, and if the person said, "I'm a Christian," they were asked on what basis they expected to go to heaven.

- 52 percent of US self-identified Christians expected to experience salvation on the basis of good works.
- 48 percent believed they would experience salvation on the basis of their confession of sin and faith in Christ.

The president of Arizona Christian University, Len Munsil, said that the "lack of understanding of basic Christian theology is stunning. . . . It's a wake-up call for the church."[4] Yet this is essentially the same thing Paul was fighting.

Let's go on to what Paul said in verse 7: "But whatever were gains to me I now consider loss for the sake of Christ."

Before Paul met Christ, he was proud of his Jewish pedigree, his strict lifestyle, his zealous work ethic, and his outward success. But the moment he met Jesus Christ on the Damascus Road, those things seemed like rubbish, like loss, compared to what he had just discovered.

Notice the word "whatever." It includes the seven virtues Paul listed, along with everything else in all of life. Now he knew the truth: *All there is in the world is worthless compared to knowing Christ.*

> **WHATEVER ARE GAINS TO US ARE LOSS COMPARED TO THE SURPASSING VALUE OF KNOWING CHRIST JESUS AS OUR LORD.**

We cannot find a life worth living through commas. We cannot accumulate enough good works or rituals or wealth or fame to have a fulfilling life. We cannot acquire enough merit points, bank accounts, personal jets, or media appearances to really satisfy us. Whatever are gains to us are loss compared to the surpassing value of knowing Christ Jesus as our Lord.

What Spurgeon Said

I wish I could say things as well as Charles Spurgeon did. God gave him an imagination and a vocabulary that never stopped. Here is what he wrote in his autobiography:

> My Christ is more precious to me than anything my fellow-creatures have. I see some who live in palaces, sit on thrones, wear crowns, and feast on dainties. I have heard of Alexanders, Napoleons, and Caesars; but I envy them not, for Christ is more precious to me than all earthly dominion.
>
> I see others with great riches. They are afraid of losing what they have, yet they are groaning after more. They have many cares through their wealth, and they must leave it all one day; but Christ is better than all earthly riches. Shall I give up Christ for gold? No, for Christ is more precious to me than wealth could ever be.
>
> Some men have noble minds; they long for knowledge, they toil that they may measure the earth, survey the heavens, read the lore of the ancients, dissolve minerals, but Christ is better to me than learning.
>
> Others pant for fame. I shall be forgotten, save by the few whose steps I have guided in the path to heaven; but I weep not at that, for Christ is more precious to me than fame. He is more precious than anything I myself have.
>
> If I have a home and fireside and feel a comfort in them, yet, if called to suffer banishment, I have a better home. If I have relatives, mother and father and faithful friends; these I value and rightly too. 'Tis a bitter pang to lose them. But Christ is better than relatives or friends. He is my Husband, my Brother, the One who loves me.
>
> I have health, and that is a precious jewel. Take it away and pleasures lose their gloss, but my Jesus is mine still, and He is better than health, yes, better than life itself.
>
> When I consider the glory of His nature, the excellence of His character, the greatness of His offices, the richness of His gifts, surely He is indeed precious. . . . To know that Christ is precious, to feel it in truth, is everything.[5]

What Jesus Said

What Paul and Spurgeon are saying was taught by Jesus Himself in embryonic form in His parables of the kingdom. He devoted two very brief parables to this.

In Matthew 13:44, He said, "The kingdom of heaven is like treasure hidden in a field. When a man found it, he hid it again, and then in his joy went and sold all he had and bought that field."

This has happened many times with the discovery of gold, precious minerals, or diamonds. Some years ago in Zambia, a prospector was out hunting and shot an antelope. As he investigated the fallen animal, he saw classic signs of copper ore in the rock next to the animal. He kept the discovery to himself, but began a frantic effort to acquire the land. It later became one of the largest copper mines in Africa.

Jesus was telling us in Matthew 13, in plain terms, "I am the only true and lasting treasure you will ever find or ever need, and it's worth everything else to follow Me."

In the next verse, He said, "The kingdom of heaven is like a merchant looking for fine pearls. When he found one of great value, he went away and sold everything he had and bought it" (vv. 5–46).

One of the richest men in the world is Philip Ng of Singapore, who is a billionaire. He recently spoke to Fox News, saying, "I was always in search for a better life, a better purpose, a better me, a better everything. I was just looking at all the wrong things, but then I realized there is no better me or better things without Jesus. Then it all snapped into place . . . I treasure my [faith in Christ] more than anything, so I just wish for everyone to have that peace and joy. It sure beats a lot of money and material things you may have."[6]

Amen. Whatever happens, value Christ above commas.

> I'd rather have Jesus than silver or gold;
> I'd rather be His than have riches untold;
> I'd rather have Jesus than houses or land;
> I'd rather be led by His nail-pierced hand

Than to be the king of a vast domain
And be held in sin's dread sway.
I'd rather have Jesus than anything
This world affords today.[7]

Sometimes we do want more of houses and land than we should, and there are moments when sin's sway doesn't seem dreadful but delightful. Nevertheless, after years of living, I can embrace this hymn.

Are you willing to make it your prayer too?

Chapter 19

WHATEVER HAPPENS . . .

GROW DEEPER EACH MORNING

(PHILIPPIANS 3:7-11)

E lizabeth Gibson was walking through New York City's Upper West Side when she saw a pile of trash. The garbage truck was just down the street, headed that way. Among the debris, she spotted a piece of canvas with a lot of colored oils on it. She pulled it from the trash, took it home, studied it, and tried to figure out what to do with it. It was too large for her small apartment, yet she loved the colors. Where had it come from? Why did it so attract her?

With the help of the *Antiques Roadshow*, she discovered it was a rare painting by a famous Mexican artist and worth over a million dollars. And yet someone had thrown it out with the trash.[1]

So many people don't know the difference between trash and treasure! The apostle Paul, however, did, and he explained it in Philippians 3, beginning with verse 7:

But whatever were gains to me I now consider loss for the sake of Christ. What is more, I consider everything a loss because of the surpassing worth of knowing Christ Jesus my Lord, for whose sake I have lost all things. I consider them garbage, that I may gain Christ and be found in him, not having a righteousness of my own that comes from the law, but that which is through faith in Christ—the righteousness that comes from God on the basis of faith. I want to know Christ—yes, to know the power of his resurrection and participation in his sufferings, becoming like him in his death, and so, somehow, attaining to the resurrection from the dead. (vv. 7–11)

I Want to Know Christ

My mother taught bookkeeping when I was in high school, and I was one of her students. She taught us about balance sheets. On one side are all our debts and liabilities. On the other side are our assets. We all have a balance sheet, whether we realize it or not, whether it's written or not. Well, in this passage, the apostle Paul took his personal balance sheet and turned it upside down. He said, "The things I thought were assets, I now consider to be liabilities, and the things I thought were liabilities, I now consider assets."

He said it quite plainly: Everything in this world is garbage compared to the surpassing worth of personally knowing Jesus Christ.

I remember the first time I heard Graham Kendrick's wonderful song "Knowing You," which is based on this passage. The closing line says, "There is no greater thing." Though it's one of those contemporary songs that comes and goes, pushed off the charts by newer songs, it's one I've never forgotten and frequently still sing.[2] Paul would have liked it too.

EVERYTHING IN THIS WORLD IS GARBAGE COMPARED TO THE SURPASSING WORTH OF PERSONALLY KNOWING JESUS CHRIST.

I recently had an interview with Sam Rohrer, president of American Pastors Network. Sam, a Pennsylvania politician, served almost two decades as a state representative in Harrisburg. He told me that the Pennsylvania capitol building is filled with scriptures, words engraved on the walls. In fact, there are fifty-nine verses etched onto the walls of that beautiful building. Sam told me he used to take people on biblical tours of the statehouse. "Let me take you on a trip through the capitol building," he would tell friends. "I can lead you to heaven through the Senate chamber."[3]

He was referring to the power of the gospel, engraved on the walls of the Senate. The only way to get to heaven is through our faith in the power of the gospel, which represents the death and resurrection of a sinless Messiah, the Lord Jesus Christ.

We hear the message of Jesus, realize that's what we need more than anything else in this world, confess our sins, place ourselves in His hands, and welcome Him into our lives as Savior and Lord. Finding Him is the most important thing in the world. Compared to that, everything else is garbage.

What the world holds in contempt, we hold in rapturous contemplation. We go back two thousand years, and there amid the smoldering ruins of a gloomy day of anguish near the trash heaps of Jerusalem, we find an old rugged cross. We find it, and with the hymn writer, we declare: "I'll cherish that old rugged cross, till our trophies at last I lay down; I will cling to that old rugged cross, and exchange it some day for a crown."[4]

I Want to Know Christ Better and Better

In verse 10, Paul went step further, talking about the lifelong process of knowing Christ better. "I want to know Christ—yes, to know the power of his resurrection and participation in his sufferings, becoming like him."

The other day I stopped in Atlanta to see Frank Fry, the man who introduced me to my wife, Katrina, half a century ago. He'd been on staff at Columbia International University, and when I returned at the beginning of my senior year, he wanted to introduce me to his new secretary. I followed him into the office, and he said, "Robert, this is Miss Polvinen." Katrina looked up and smiled, and I remember that moment clearly in my mind. I don't fully know why. Over the last half-century, I've met thousands of people I can't remember, but I clearly remember meeting her though I had no idea I had just met my future wife.

If someone had asked me the next day if I knew Katrina, I would have said, "Yes, I met her yesterday." But did I really know her yet? Our momentary meeting was only the beginning of the process of getting to know each other. Doing so involved working together that year, building a friendship, and later falling in love, getting married, and building a home together.

It's that way with Jesus Christ. There comes a day when we meet Him by receiving Him as our Savior and Lord. But for the rest of our lives and for all eternity, we'll be getting to know Him better and better.

How do we do that?

Through Fellowship with Him

It's like getting to know another person better. It happens through conversation, through fellowship, through spending time together. As a young man, I bought a copy of the Amplified Bible and began reading the book of Philippians. When I came to Philippians 3:10, it changed the way I understood the concept of knowing God. I memorized this verse from that translation and have gone back to it again and again:

> [For my determined purpose is] that I may know Him [that I may progressively become more deeply and intimately acquainted with Him, perceiving and recognizing and understanding the wonders of His Person more strongly and more clearly]. (AMPC)

The translators took that one word—*know*—and used twenty-seven words to define it.

Knowing Christ means to progressively become more deeply and intimately acquainted with Him. The primary way of doing that is through daily conversation with Him, which happens through daily Bible study and prayer. Those simple concepts have shaped my ministry, and I've done everything in my power to help people meet Christ at the cross and then meet with Him each day for prayer and Bible study.

Years ago, I prepared a sermon called "The Cross and the Closet." In older translations of the Bible, Jesus said in Matthew 6:6 that we should go into our closet and pray to our heavenly Father. In those days, most houses were small and filled with children and animals. But there was always a small room for supplies. Jesus told us to find that private place where we can be alone with God.

In my sermon, I said that we meet Christ originally at the cross, and we call that conversion. But then we meet with Him daily in the closet, and we call that conversation. At the cross, we come to know Him. And in the closet, we come to know Him better and better.

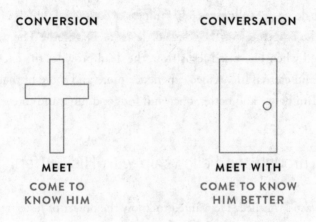

CONVERSION	CONVERSATION
MEET	**MEET WITH**
COME TO KNOW HIM	COME TO KNOW HIM BETTER

Through the Power of His Resurrection

Let's look at Paul's words in verse 10 again: "I want to know Christ—yes, to know the power of his resurrection."

I believe the Holy Spirit had something to do with the ordering and the arrangement of the books of the Bible. Philippians follows Ephesians, and it seems to me Paul was referring to what he wrote just a few pages earlier in Ephesians 1:17–20: "I keep asking that the God of our Lord Jesus Christ, the glorious Father, may give you the Spirit of wisdom and revelation, so that you may know him better. I pray . . . that you may know . . . his incomparably great power

AT THE CROSS, WE COME TO KNOW HIM. AND IN THE CLOSET, WE COME TO KNOW HIM BETTER AND BETTER.

for us who believe. That power is the same as the mighty strength he exerted when he raised Christ from the dead and seated him at his right hand in the heavenly realms."

Did you catch it? The same power that fueled the resurrection of Jesus Christ from the dead is available to fuel our daily living. And we're to live in that resurrection power.

Recently I was in Jerusalem with my grandson Elijah visiting the garden tomb. It was dark, but path lights led to the sepulchre, which was dimly lit. As we stood there in the dim light of an empty ancient grave, this thought came to me: *The only way to live in fullness is to live in emptiness.*

Where do we get fullness of joy? Fullness of courage? Fullness of the Spirit? It's from the emptiness of the tomb of Jesus of Nazareth. The same power God exerted when He raised Jesus from the dead provides the energy for our abundant and eternal life. As we experience more and more of that, we come to know Him better and better, once and for good, now and forever.

Through the Fellowship with His Suffering

But Paul wasn't finished. He wanted to know the power of Jesus' resurrection, but there was more. In verse 10, he continued, "I want to know . . . his sufferings, becoming like him in his death." We come to know Christ more deeply through fellowship with His suffering and death. As we faithfully serve Him, we may encounter opposition, hostility, and persecution. That enables us to experience a bit of what Christ experienced, and it causes us to trust Him more than ever.

It's strange how the world hates Christianity. I listened to a fascinating interview Shane Morris conducted with Christian thinker Frederica Mathewes-Green. As a young adult, Frederica was part of the counterculture, a feminist hippie, but something bothered her. She realized in college that she had contempt for Christians but not for the adherents of other religions. She admired Hinduism. She admired aspects of all the other religions. But she realized she hated Christians to the point of wanting to embarrass or humiliate them. And she began to wonder where that was coming from.

That nagging question began to convict her, and over time it led her to investigate Christianity and to become a deeply devoted follower of Christ.[5]

Jesus said, "If you belonged to the world, it would love you as its own. As it is, you do not belong to the world, but I have chosen you out of the world. That is why the world hates you" (John 15:19).

We're essentially a different race of people from everyone else. We are citizens of another kingdom, we serve a different King—and the world instinctively has contempt for us. As we realize that and even experience it, we become more like Christ as we share in the contempt He faced. And that's how we grow closer to Him.

I Want to Know Christ Throughout Eternity

We want to come to know Christ; we grow to know Him better; and then we want to continue to grow in our knowledge of Him throughout eternity. Notice what Paul said next: "I want to know Christ . . . and so, somehow, [attain] to the resurrection from the dead."

This word "somehow" doesn't imply doubt but wonder. Paul wasn't saying, "Somehow I hope I'll be resurrected." He was saying, "I am amazed by the thought that Almighty God in His triumphant power will somehow bring all the molecules of my decayed body together at His return, and I'll be resurrected."

That's when we'll continue getting to know Christ.

In His great and final prayer in John 17, Jesus prayed: "Father, I want those you have given me to be with me where I am, and to see my glory" (v. 24). In other words, the Lord Jesus wants us to be with Him forever, beholding Him with growing awe and wonder. Revelation 22:4 says we will see His face.

We will have a literal infinity of time to walk with Him, to talk with Him, to be with Him, to fellowship with Him. There will be billions of people in heaven, but because of the nature of everlasting life, we will have endless opportunities to spend time with Him. We'll get to know Him better and better and better. I'll say more about this in the next chapter, but for now let me leave you with Paul's words in Philippians 3:10 from the Amplified Bible Classic Edition:

[For my determined purpose is] that I may know Him [that I may progressively become more deeply and intimately acquainted with Him, perceiving and recognizing and understanding the wonders of His Person more strongly and more clearly].

Chapter 20

WHATEVER HAPPENS . . .

ACTIVELY PRESS ON

(PHILIPPIANS 3:12-14)

Somewhere I picked up an autographed copy of a book by Meb Keflezighi, the marathon champion. It's entitled *26 Marathons*. Meb describes each of his twenty-six legendary marathon races—26 races of 26.2 miles each—and what he learned along the way. Meb came to America from war-torn Eretria and is a Christ follower. About his winning the 2009 New York City Marathon, he said, "I've always believed consistency, not isolated killer workouts, is the key to peak performance. Many elite runners could have done any one day or even any one week of my training for New York. It's doing those days and weeks over and over again that makes the difference."[1]

Well, in his thirteen amazing letters, the apostle Paul often used racing as a metaphor. We have to be consistently running, training, and making progress. Philippians 3:12–14 is all about this.

> Not that I have already obtained all this, or have already arrived at my goal,
> but I press on to take hold of that for which Christ Jesus took hold of me.
> Brothers and sisters, I do not consider myself yet to have taken hold of it.

But one thing I do: Forgetting what is behind and straining toward what is ahead, I press on toward the goal to win the prize for which God has called me heavenward in Christ Jesus.

Paul began chapter 3 by warning us against false teachers. In his day, his primary opponents were the Judaizers. Paul said that in terms of Jewish heritage, they had nothing on his impeccable Jewishness. But, he said, those things were nothing more than rubbish compared to the surpassing value of knowing Christ.

Knowing Christ is the theme of this chapter, and what a theme it is!

The surpassing worth of knowing Christ Jesus our Lord is worth more than all the money in the world, more than all the gilded mansions in St. Petersburg, more than all the real estate in Manhattan, more than all the fame of every celebrity, more than all the precious stones in the world—all crammed into one immense treasure chest.

> **KNOWING CHRIST JESUS OUR LORD IS WORTH MORE THAN ALL THE MONEY IN THE WORLD.**

Everything is garbage and rubbish compared with the surpassing value of knowing Christ our Lord.

Here in the heart of chapter 3, Paul defined three distinct phases of knowing Christ. Let's take a young couple in love. First, they meet each other and begin dating. Second, they become engaged; and third, they get married. In every stage, the goal is to get to know each other better.

Paul used these same terms to describe the process of experiencing the surpassing value of knowing Christ: First we gain Christ (v. 8), then we get to know Christ (v. 10), and finally we are called heavenward to be with Christ (v. 14). Let's unpack those three steps.

Gaining Christ

I've often encouraged people to *receive* Christ or *accept* Christ. But Paul talked about *gaining* Christ. The Greek term, *lambano*, implies acquisition. This refers to the moment when we receive Jesus Christ as our Savior.

Recently the Gideons International gave me a book telling about their hundred-plus years of ministry, and in it I read about Orel Hershiser, who spent seventeen years as a professional baseball player. After he signed with the Los Angeles Dodgers in 1979, he was assigned to training camp in Scottsdale, Arizona. His teammate and roommate was a dedicated Christian who was always reading his Bible. One night, Hershiser asked him what he saw in that old book, and his roommate said, "Everything."

Shortly afterward, Hershiser picked up the Gideon Bible in his room, started reading it, and came under deep conviction. He later said, "Without any prompting, I slipped to my knees by the bed. Openly confessing my sins, I invited Christ into my life."[2]

I later read that he loved to sing the doxology. He sang it in the locker room, in the dugout, and even on *The Tonight Show Starring Johnny Carson*. Orel could praise God from whom all blessings flow because he had gained Christ.

At some point we all need to slip to our knees, confess our sins, and invite Jesus into our lives as Savior and Lord. That's how we meet Christ. That's how we begin the process of getting to know Him.

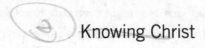 Knowing Christ

There's a second phase and a second phrase here: *knowing Christ*. Look again at verses 8–10, and notice the words I've emphasized:

> . . . that I may *gain Christ* and be found in him, not having a righteousness of my own that comes from the law, but that which is through faith in Christ—the righteousness that comes from God on the basis of faith. I want to *know Christ*.

Paul said, "I have gained Christ; now I want to know Him." It was time to get to know Him better—to become more intimately and deeply acquainted with Him. This happens over the course of our lifetime as we cultivate our friendship with Him.

Hosea 6:3 (ESV) says: "Let us know; let us press on to know the LORD; his going out is sure as the dawn; he will come to us as the showers, as the spring rains that water the earth."

An article in *Women's Health* magazine recently suggested two hundred questions to ask to get to know someone better. Questions included: What do you like to do on your day off? What was the best vacation you ever had? What are your hobbies? If you could change anything about yourself, would you?[3]

Of course, it's not a matter of sitting down and going through the list of questions. The idea is that getting to know someone involves engaging in meaningful conversation with a real desire to know that person better.

For the Christian, that's the function of what I call quiet time. Lifeway Research released the results of a survey in which they found that nearly two-thirds of all churchgoers have a daily time when they meet with God. The question on the survey was: How often do you intentionally spend time alone with God? Sixty-five percent of churchgoers said they did this daily.[4]

I was encouraged by that statistic, but I wondered if there was genuine depth behind it.

Have you noticed God speaking to you when you close the door and read your Bible? Do you look for what He might be trying to tell you? Praying is speaking to God, letting Him know the things that are on your mind. As you develop a daily habit of doing this, you will get to know Him better. That is not a shallow spot of time; it is the deepest and richest thing anyone can do.

Called Heavenward in Christ

As the years pass and we find Him faithful to us in every situation, we come to trust Him more. Our relationship with Christ should become deeper, more enjoyable, and more fulfilling as long as we live. But we have one enormous hindrance that keeps us from knowing Christ as perfectly as we'd like.

We are separated from Him by realm. We're in one realm, and He's in another. Right now we cannot see His face.

First Peter 1:8 says, "Though you have not seen him, you love him; and even though you do not see him now, you believe in him and are filled with an inexpressible and glorious joy."

Second Corinthians 5:6–8 says: "As long as we are at home in the body we are away from the Lord. For we live by faith, not by sight. We are confident, I say, and would prefer to be away from the body and at home with the Lord."

We know Him now through the blessing of salvation, through the Scriptures, and through the Holy Spirit in our hearts and lives. Dr. Gordon Fee wrote that the Holy Spirit represents the presence of God and of Christ among us now. "The Spirit," he said, "is the way God is present now."

In the Old Testament, God the Father dwelled among His people of Israel as a cloud of glory in the holy of holies. He also represented the Son and the Spirit.

In the Gospels, God the Son dwelled among His people in His flesh. He also represented the Father and the Spirit.

On the day of Pentecost, God the Spirit came to dwell among His people, and here He remains, representing the Father and the Son. Paul referred to the Holy Spirit 145 times in his thirteen letters.[5]

The Holy Spirit dwells in and around us. He seals us, fills us, and empowers us. He strengthens us in our inner being. He cultivates the character of Jesus within us. The love of God is poured into our hearts by the Holy Spirit. We are led by the Spirit, and we overflow with hope through the power of the Holy Spirit. When we engage in service and ministry, it is the power of the Holy Spirit within us who is accomplishing the results.

Ephesians 1:17 says: "I keep asking that the God of our Lord Jesus Christ, the glorious Father, may give you the [Holy] Spirit of wisdom and revelation, so that you may know him better."

Katrina and I fell in love long distance. After I graduated from Columbia International University, I moved to Chicago to attend Wheaton College Graduate School. Katrina was still in South Carolina. We knew each other and had worked together, but we didn't think of ourselves as in love. In those days we didn't have cell phones, only pay phones, and calls were hard to coordinate. We wrote letters to each other instead, and we fell in love through our letters.

It's possible to get to know and fall in love with someone even if you can't see his or her face. In the case of Jesus, it's by the agency of the Holy Spirit and Scripture and prayer. But one day we will see Him face-to-face.

I believe that's what Paul was talking about in Philippians 3:14. The Amplified Bible Classic Edition says, "I press on toward the goal to win the [supreme and heavenly] prize to which God in Christ Jesus is calling us upward."

Heavenward, upward, skyward. The prize is being with Jesus forever.

Paul wanted to be as close to Christ as he could possibly be. He had gained Him as his Savior. He was growing in love with Him through the Holy Spirit and getting to know Him better. He was straining and pressing on—without looking back—for that day when God would call him heavenward, upward. And when that day came, Paul knew he would see Jesus face-to-face.

When Stephen was being stoned to death for his faith, he said, "Look! I see the heavens opened and the Son of Man standing at the right hand of God!" (Acts 7:56 NKJV).

In 1 Corinthians 13:12, Paul said, "For now we see in a mirror, dimly, but then face to face. Now I know in part, but then I shall know just as I also am known" (NKJV).

In Philippians 1:23, Paul said, "I am torn between the two: I desire to depart and be with Christ, which is better by far."

First John 3:2 says, "We know that when Christ appears, we shall be like him, for we shall see him as he is."

Revelation 22:3–4 says, "The throne of God and of the Lamb will be in the city, and his servants will serve him. They will see his face."

These are the stages of our relationship with Christ, which I first touched on back in chapter 5. We gain Christ when we receive Him as Savior—that's justification. We get to know Him better as we walk in the Spirit—that's sanctification or Christification. One day we will see Him face-to-face—that's glorification.

Oh, to see the face of Christ—as bright as the sunshine, as wise as He is omniscient, as full of smiles as He is full of grace. And then we'll have all eternity to be with Him, to walk with Him, to talk with Him, to dine with Him, and to see the wonders of His majesty.

That's why, like championship runners, we are straining and striving to win the prize for the upward call of God in Christ Jesus. You know by now I'm a lover of hymns and Christian songs, and it's hard for me to study a passage like this without thinking of a song like "It Will Be Worth It All When We See Jesus."

If you grow weary, think of that. All the trials of life take on a different perspective when we think of that moment when we first see His face. Your burdens aren't eternal, but your blessings are. Your load won't always be so heavy, but your Lord will be dearer to you as the eons pass. So run your race until the day when you visibly, literally, wonderfully see His blessed smile.

Chapter 21

WHATEVER HAPPENS . . .

BE CAREFUL WHO YOU ADMIRE

(PHILIPPIANS 3:17-21)

I recently read about a group of men who wanted to hike a rugged portion of the Buffalo National River that winds through the Ozarks. It's a dramatic area controlled by the National Park Service (NPS). There are no dams on the river, and some spots are treacherous with sheer, breathtaking bluffs. One of the men fell to his death. The NPS said the reason was the group hired a guide who didn't have a license or insurance, nor did he have a good track record. He took their money, then led them into an area that exceeded their level of preparation.

A man died because he followed the wrong guide. How easily that happens in life.

Paul addressed this in Philippians 3:17–19:

Join together in following my example, brothers and sisters, and just as you have us as a model, keep your eyes on those who live as we do. For, as I have often told you before and now tell you again even with tears, many live as enemies of the cross of Christ. Their destiny is destruction, their god is their stomach, and their glory is in their shame. Their mind is set on earthly things.

Look for People Who Can Strengthen You

Notice in verse 17, Paul told us we will only find a few people in this world after whom we should pattern our lives. I would suggest the entire letter to the Philippians hinges on this thought.

As we've noted before, the first twenty-six verses of Philippians are an extended introduction in which Paul told us what and how he was doing. The actual formal content in the letter begins in Philippians 1:27: "Whatever happens, conduct yourselves in a manner worthy of the gospel of Christ. Then, whether I come and see you or only hear about you in my absence, I will know that you stand firm." That's the theme of chapter 1: Whatever happens, I want you to stand firm.

In chapter 2, Paul gave us Jesus as an example and told us to have the mind of Christ. He also held up Timothy and Epaphroditus as examples for us. Then in chapter 3, he offered himself as an example, telling us to model ourselves after him. Paul finished the formal content of his letter in chapter 4:1 by saying: "This is how you must stand firm in the Lord." That's the sequence of the letter: Stand firm—like Jesus, like Timothy, like Epaphroditus, like me—*stand firm*.

STAND FIRM— LIKE JESUS, LIKE TIMOTHY, LIKE EPAPHRODITUS, LIKE ME—*STAND FIRM*.

Today, when the forces coming against the followers of Christ are relentless, the Lord wants us to stand firm for the truth. In doing so, we must stand firm against:

- our own fallen natures with their tendencies to sin and bitterness and division,
- the culture: sexual immorality, pornography, the vile nature of our society,
- the efforts of our enemies to intimidate us or persuade us to compromise our biblical worldview,
- the theological errors of the false teachers and the erosion of doctrine in our churches, and
- the attitudes of fear and hopelessness that can plunder our joy.

It's vital that we find men and women who are standing firm, who are holding to the apostolic faith, who are victorious, who are joyful and biblical, and who have developed the habits and attitudes of true Christianity. We need their examples.

Do you have someone in your life who provides you such a pattern? I'm thankful the Lord gave me some great mentors, from my parents to my pastors to my professors and others. I sometimes had to seek them out, and I had to have a teachable spirit. I'm not beyond needing people like that now. Sometimes I find them through their writings. I never met Elisabeth Elliot, but I almost always have an Elisabeth Elliot book nearby. Often when I feel downcast, a page or two of Elisabeth can set me right.

Avoid People Who Can Mess You Up

The next thing Paul told us is this: While we'll only find a few people living apostolically and biblically to follow, we'll find a large number of people who will mess up our lives very quickly, and we must avoid being influenced by them in any way. Paul described these people in five ways in verses 18–19:

1. They are enemies of the cross of Christ, hostile to the message of Scripture and to the gospel.
2. Their destiny is destruction. They are hell-bound, in direct contrast to what Paul just said about himself earlier in chapter 3, that he is straining forward toward the upward call of God in Christ.
3. Their god is their stomach. They're controlled by appetites and desires.
4. Their glory is in their shame. They're proud of what they should be ashamed of.
5. They set their minds on earthly things. They don't study the Bible or ponder the truth of the Lord or the things of God. They don't think about heaven. They are absorbed with this fleeting earth.

I don't need to elaborate because this is the world that surrounds us every day. These are the people that populate our culture.

Follow the One Who Can Transform You

Now Paul arrived at the climax of his argument. If we're going to stand firm in our faith, there are a few people whom we should emulate and many people we should avoid, but there is only one Man to whom we should give our lives and who can transform us forever. Look at verses 20 and 21:

> But our citizenship is in heaven. And we eagerly await a Savior from there, the Lord Jesus Christ, who, by the power that enables him to bring every-thing under his control, will transform our lowly bodies so that they will be like his glorious body.

This is acknowledged by theologians and Bible students alike to be one of the greatest eschatological passages in all the Bible. Paul didn't say, "Our citizenship will be in heaven." We are *now* currently citizens of heaven, living as expatriates here on earth. I remember hearing Vance Havner say, "We are not citizens of earth going to heaven; we are citizens of heaven traveling through earth."[1]

When I travel overseas, whether I am in France or England or Ghana or Japan, my thoughts are back home. I'm glad to be of service in those countries for a little while, and I enjoy seeing the sites. But I miss my family and don't feel totally at home in the various cultures I visit. The stress and strain of travel get to me.

The book of Hebrews says we are "foreigners and strangers on earth" (11:13). First Peter 1:17 tell us to "live out your time as foreigners here in reverent fear."

If you want me to prove I'm an American, I'll pull out my passport. But if you want me to prove I'm a citizen of heaven, I'll pull out my Bible and turn to Philippians 3:20. Our citizenship is in heaven. It is recorded in heaven, and we are under the jurisdiction and constitutional protection of heaven. The very

King of heaven is our Father. "And we eagerly await a Savior from there, the Lord Jesus Christ."

As I've studied the four chapters of Philippians, I've found twelve references to the return of Christ and our eternal home.[2] For example, Paul said in chapter 1 that for him, to live is Christ and to die is gain. He desired to depart and be with Christ, which is far better. In chapter 2, he talked about the day when every knee will bow and every tongue will confess that Christ is Lord. In chapter 3, he talked about the upward call of God in Christ, and finally, in chapter 4, he reminded his readers that the Lord is near. Many people interpret that to mean that the Lord's *coming* is near.

As you study his thirteen epistles, you'll discover that Paul could hardly write a chapter without talking about the return of Christ and our eternal home. After all, he'd been caught up to the third heaven and had seen just a little bit of what awaits us there. He said he'd heard inexpressible things while in paradise that he was not permitted to tell (2 Corinthians 12:1–4).

Every sunrise reminded Paul of the coming of the Son of Man in clouds of glory. Every sunset reminded him he was one day closer to that event. Every time he looked up to the sky, he thought of heaven beyond. Every time he looked down at the ground, he thought of how very temporary his stay here was. Every goodbye reminded him of the coming reunion where there would be no more sad partings, and every pain he felt reminded him of the day when pain would be no more. Every brush with death gave him a thrill of being nearer to heaven, and every act of service reminded him that his labor on earth was nearly over.

The last thought in chapter 3 looks again at the coming Savior whom we eagerly await and "who, by the power that enables him to bring everything under his control, will transform our lowly bodies so that they will be like his glorious body" (v. 21).

If you have been redeemed by the blood of Christ, one day you will be resurrected, transformed, and glorified according to the observable pattern of the resurrected and glorified body of Jesus Christ. I've studied this in the Scripture and I've not been able to exhaustively understand it, but let me give you three facts I do understand.

ONE DAY YOU WILL BE RESURRECTED, TRANSFORMED, AND GLORIFIED ACCORDING TO THE OBSERVABLE PATTERN OF THE RESURRECTED AND GLORIFIED BODY OF JESUS CHRIST.

1. Our Resurrection Bodies Will Be Recognizable

The resurrection body will be our actual bodies—the ones we have currently here on earth—and not a new creation. As I was working on this book, a friend sent me a question about whether we would really know our loved ones in heaven. The answer is yes. We will be identifiable in our new bodies. We will recognize each other. Jesus was alive in the same physical body that had been crucified. They recognized Him, and He spoke to them with His mouth and with His voice—the same voice they had known and loved. And they fell at His feet and wrapped their arms around His ankles. We'll have the same recognizable bodies we have on earth. You will be a new and improved version, but you will still be you.

2. Our Resurrection Bodies Will Be Functional

They will function very much like our current bodies. Luke 24:36–43 shows us Jesus' freshly resurrected body on the evening of the original Easter Sunday:

> While they were still talking about this, Jesus himself stood among them and said to them, "Peace be with you." They were startled and frightened, thinking they had seen a ghost. He said to them, "Why are you troubled, and why do doubts rise in your minds? Look at my hands and my feet. It is I myself! Touch me and see; a ghost does not have flesh and bones, as you see I have."
>
> When he had said this, he showed them his hands and feet. And while they still did not believe it because of joy and amazement, he asked them, "Do you have anything here to eat?" They gave him a piece of broiled fish, and he took it and ate it in their presence.

We'll be able to eat. In heaven, we'll enjoy eating and drinking just as we do on earth. There's no reason I can think of that we shouldn't also be involved in food preparation if we want. I happen to enjoy cooking, but in heaven know I'll not give anyone food poisoning when they come over to my place for lunch.

Jesus did remarkable things with His resurrected body. He could appear and disappear; He could pass through stone barriers and wooden doorways; He could apparently travel by telepathy. Will we be able to do those things, or are they unique to His divinity? I can't speculate, but I do know our bodies will be far more functional than they are now.

3. Our Resurrection Bodies Will Be Imperishable

The most extensive passage on this subject is 1 Corinthians 15. In a way, Philippians 3:21 is a one-verse summary of the entire fifteenth chapter of 1 Corinthians. The first part of the chapter talks about the resurrection of Christ, and then Paul progressed to talk about the subsequent resurrection of Christ's followers. Verse 42 says: "The body that is sown is perishable, it is raised imperishable."

Our glorified bodies will never be capable of deterioration, and that means no sickness, no weakness, no exhaustion, no disease, no aging, no dying, no surgeries, no drugs.

And that's why Paul said in Philippians 4:1: "Therefore, my brothers and sisters, you whom I love and long for, my joy and crown, stand firm in the Lord in this way, dear friends."

There are a few people who are worth emulating today. There are many more who will mess up our lives if we let them. But there is only one person who has the power to bring all things under His authority and transform us forever. We are citizens of His kingdom—and we are eagerly awaiting His glorious return, when He will rapture the living, raise the dead in Christ, and transform our lowly bodies so they become like His glorious body.

Whatever happens today or tomorrow, don't worry. Follow the right guide. Follow the one who invites you to come, deny yourself, take up your cross, and follow Him.

Chapter 22

WHATEVER HAPPENS . . .

PROJECT YOURSELF INTO THE FUTURE

(PHILIPPIANS 3:20-21)

Anticipation keeps me going. What about you? Do you feel the need to look forward to what's ahead—a vacation, a weekend at the beach or in the mountains, the birth of a child or grandchild, the diploma that concludes your studies, the day you retire, or even the fresh taste of tomatoes in summer?

Over the past five years, I've grappled with three tremendous losses. Because of my wife's multiple sclerosis, I stepped away from my life's work of pastoring. That was a greater loss than I realized at the time. Sometime later, Katrina passed away. And then my dream of serving in my own local church of forty years evaporated. I was no longer needed.

For months, my thoughts troubled me during the day and my dreams at night. And then the Lord gave me two verses of Scripture that spoke clearly to my weary soul. Isaiah 43:18–19 says:

> "Forget the former things;
> do not dwell on the past.
> See, I am doing a new thing!

Now it springs up; do you not perceive it?
I am making a way in the wilderness
and streams in the [desert]."[1]

A few months later, my grandson Elijah and I visited Israel and went hiking in En Gedi. This is a curious valley in a barren wilderness. All around this gorge, everything is hot and desolate. The distant Hebron mountains to the west, made of limestone, soak up the rain like a reservoir. That water travels a long way through underground fissures, all the way out to the rocks of En Gedi. There, water surges like fire hydrants. Splashing waterfalls cascade through the valley. There are streams in the desert, and it seemed as though the Lord was saying, "See, this is what I'm talking about."

That passage in Isaiah—"Forget the former things; do not dwell on the past. See, I am doing a new thing"—reminds me of Paul's words in Philippians 3:13–14: "Forgetting what is behind and straining toward what is ahead, I press on toward the goal to win the prize for which God has called me heavenward in Christ Jesus."

We should always exercise future-oriented therapy—the biblical practice of knowing our best days are ahead and that even after this life, we have the certain hope of heaven and the resurrection body.

Why don't we dwell on these things more? Why aren't we more excited every day about the glorious future God has revealed to us in His Word? We get so caught up in the *here and now* that we forget the *then and there*.

The contemplation of our future inheritance in Christ, our heavenly home, our glorious reunion with the saints of all the ages, and our mansions in the new earth and in the city of New Jerusalem would save us from much of the despair and depression that dogs us here on earth.

Philippians 3:20–21 is one of the Bible's great statements about this: "Our citizenship is in heaven. And we eagerly await a Savior from there, the Lord Jesus Christ, who, by the power that enables him to bring everything under his control, will transform our lowly bodies so that they will be like his glorious body."

Let's think about that day. First Thessalonians 4:16–17 says, "The Lord Himself will descend from heaven with a shout, with the voice of an archangel, and with the trumpet of God. And the dead in Christ will rise first. Then we who are alive *and* remain shall be caught up together with them in the clouds to meet the Lord in the air" (NKJV).

In 1 Corinthians 15:42–44, Paul talked at length about how the body that is sown into the earth as a perishable object will be raised imperishable and incorruptible. First John 3:2 says that when we see Him, we will be like Him.

I've studied this subject for a long time, but recently I found a sermon from yesteryear that paints a vivid picture of our glorious resurrection bodies. The preacher was Samuel Dunn, a Methodist pastor who wrote extensively.

On Sunday, October 16, 1842, in the South Parade Chapel in Halifax, England, Dunn delivered a sermon titled "The Glorified Body." As I read his sermon, I could imagine the good pastor standing in his quaint pulpit and sharing these words in his engaging British enunciation.

> As Christ is risen from the dead; as He has destroyed the destroyer, spoiled the grave, burst the barriers of the tomb, opened the iron gates of death, our resurrection will follow. He rose in our nature, as our representative. His resurrection was a proof, a pledge, an earnest of ours. . . . The resurrection will be a miraculous work, performed by Christ. "As in Adam all die, even so in Christ will all be made alive" [1 Corinthians 15:22 KJV].

Rev. Dunn went on to admit how perplexing it is to imagine how our bodies, reduced by time to dust to be blown in the wind and washed away in the flood, could be reclaimed, reconstituted, and resurrected and we still retain our same identity. "But He who first formed it from the dust of the earth is able to do it," he said. "To omnipotence, it is possible—it is easy."

Those who have fallen asleep in Christ, as the apostle Paul put it, will yet be fearfully and wonderfully made, in the moment of our resurrection as in the moment of our conception. Dunn continued:

> The body . . . is the most beautiful and curious piece of mechanism that was ever constructed. The dignity of its form, the symmetry of its parts, the

WE GET SO CAUGHT UP IN THE *HERE AND NOW* THAT WE FORGET THE *THEN AND THERE*.

nature of its different organs, the relations which they bear to each other and to external objects, all show the hand of a divine architect. But in its present state it is subject to numberless infirmities. There is a constant tendency to disease. Some diseases disfigure the body, others torture it, while others rapidly corrupt its solids and poison its fluids. No powers of medicine, no skill of physicians, can preserve it in perpetual existence. . . . Death takes hold of the frame. It is screwed up in a coffin, consigned to the grave, and speedily becomes a mass of nauseous, putrid matter. It sees corruption.

But not for long. As soon as the voice of the Son of God shall strike its ear, the body will awaken, molecule joining molecule, reversing the dying process, and being remade through resurrection into a body that will "no more be subject to pain, disease, decay, mutilation, disruption, dissolution, disorganization, degradation, putrefaction."

Its substance will be indestructible and unchangeable, its inheritance incorruptible, undefiled, and will never fade away. There will be no more hostile attacks, infectious particles, unwholesome sweats, poisonous threats, or malignant vapors conspiring to its destruction. It will be no more flushed with fever or with consumption, suffocated with asthma or strangled with infection, swollen with dropsy or racked with rheumatism. . . . It shall flourish in immortal youth, in undecaying luster, ever beautiful and ever young.

The Bible teaches that "God shall wipe away all tears from their eyes; and there shall be no more death, neither sorrow, nor crying, neither shall there be any more pain: for the former things are passed way" (Revelation 21:4 KJV). Our eyesight will be enhanced to absorb the splendor of heaven's light. Our ears will be tuned to catch the song of the angels. Our strength will be like Samson's, our gentleness like a hummingbird, our wisdom greater than Solomon's, and our joy as high as the distant peaks.

Rev. Dunn continued,

The glorified body of Christ will be the model after which the bodies of His people shall be formed. . . . We shall not only see Him; we shall be like Him. The first glimpse we see of Him as we come forth from the tomb will

be a transforming one. A powerful influence shall emanate from His efful-
gence, which shall have an immediate and necessary effect of assimilating
us into His likeness. Our glorified body shall be like His, as it appeared on
the Mount of Transfiguration, when its glory so irradiated His garments
that they became as white as snow. Like His, as Saul beheld it on his way to
Damascus, when its brightness eclipsed the light of the noonday sun. Like
His, as represented to John in Patmos, when His head and His hairs were
white like wool, as white as snow, His eyes as a flame of fire and His coun-
tenance as the sun shining in all its strength.

As I read Rev. Dunn's sermon, I got a glimpse of the future me. Right
now, I'm sometimes bowed down with care, sick with viruses, and aging at an
alarming rate. Yes, so are you.

But the splendor of the resurrection body surpasses all our conceptions. It
shall be in glory—fairer than the fairest flower, purer than the unspotted
firmament, brighter than the morning star, more radiant than the midday
sun, more splendid than Adam's body in paradise, more illustrious than
angels. It shall be like the body of our Lord Jesus Christ. . . . Your risen body
will possess the power of moving, perhaps, from world to world with greater
speed than the sunbeams and with greater ease than we can now pass from
the chapel to our respective houses.

As the bodies of Enoch and Elijah and of our Lord went up into heaven,
so shall the bodies of all the saints, unaffected by the laws of gravitation or
by the pressures of the atmosphere. We shall have the power of adapting
them to every employment. The eye may have the power of seeing minute
objects immensely distant, and the ear of catching the faintest sounds. We
shall move without weariness, cogitate without exhaustion, contemplate the
loftiest objects without difficulty.

If the body shall be so glorious, how great must be the glory of the soul.[2]

Had I been in that service, I think I would have shouted "Amen!" Our
problems are all temporary, but God's promises are eternal. They will outlive

our days, outlast our trials, and outwit our weaknesses. They will carry us through time into eternity, from earth into heaven. They will produce for us all God has for us, and our future is so much better than anything we've yet experienced, far better than anything we've seen in past eras of life.

So project yourself into the future and claim God's promise of Isaiah 43:18–19:

> Forget the former things;
> do not dwell on the past.
> See, I am doing a new thing! Now it springs up; do you not
>   perceive it?
> I am making a way in the wilderness
> and streams in the [wasteland].[3]

Chapter 23

WHATEVER HAPPENS . . .

STAND FIRM

(PHILIPPIANS 4:1)

Earlier this year we had a tremendous windstorm at our house. I live on the crest of a hill, and sometimes the winds sweep up the hillside with incredible force. From my office window that day, I watched the small pine trees in my garden sway back and forth like punching bags. As a child, I had a little inflatable character I could punch in the face, sending him all the way to the floor, but he was designed to always bounce back. Those pine trees reminded me of that fellow. They held firm. They kept bouncing back because they were well rooted.

After the storm I went around to check the rest of my property. I found two larger pine trees that had not been so fortunate. They were lying on their sides with half their roots above the ground. I've had to turn them into firewood. They did not stand firm in the storm.

Many people believe that the key thought in Philippians is joy. The subject of joy is certainly a subtheme of the book, but the body of Philippians begins and ends with the idea of standing firm. This is worth noticing.

After an extended introduction, Paul began the core content of his book in Philippians 1:27: "Whatever happens, conduct yourselves in a manner worthy of the gospel of Christ. Then, whether I come and see you or only hear about you in my absence, I will know that you *stand firm* in the one Spirit" (emphasis mine).

In chapter 2 he gave us the examples of Jesus Christ, Timothy, and Epaphroditus.

In chapter 3, Paul offered himself as a resolute spiritual athlete, pressing toward the upward goal. He said, "Just as you have us as a model, keep your eyes on those who live as we do" (3:17).

Then in chapter 4, he ended the body of the book by coming full circle in verse 1 and saying, "Therefore, my brothers and sisters, you whom I love and long for, my joy and crown, *stand firm* in the Lord in this way, dear friends" (emphasis mine).

Matthew Harmon, in his excellent commentary on Philippians, agrees with my understanding of the structure of the letter. He says, "Just as Paul began the main letter body by expressing his desire to hear that the Philippians are standing firm in one Spirit (1:27), he now closes the main letter body with a final call to stand firm in the Lord (4:1)."[1]

I'm a book lover from childhood, and I appreciate the commentaries I have on various books of the Bible. I've tried over the years to select one or two top-rated commentaries for every book of the Bible. (For the book of Philippians, my favorites are by Gordon Fee and Matthew Harmon.) I've also accumulated a historical selection of books, telling the stories of world history, American history, and Christian history.

I have books on many other subjects, but my most enjoyable books are biographies and autobiographies. One whole wall of my library is devoted to them. Now I'm having to resort to electronic books because I don't have any more space.

Apart from my Bible and my hymnbook, nothing has enabled me to stand firm more than the stirring examples of the courageous saints of all the ages.

Two of our earliest heroes are Polycarp and Ignatius, who descended directly from the apostles. Both were martyred. We have a letter from Ignatius to Polycarp, exhorting him, "Stand firm, as does an anvil which is beaten. It is the part of a noble athlete to be wounded and yet to conquer. And especially we ought to bear all things for the sake of God, that He also may bear with us. Be ever more zealous than you are. Weigh carefully the times. Look to Him who is above all time, eternal and invisible."[2]

I've reveled in the *Confessions of Saint Augustine*, who prayed, "You are a stronghold and my refuge; let me flee to You, that I may grow strong in every respect where I have grown weak in myself. The grace of Christ makes [me] stand firm and immovable."

John Knox was a fearless fighter for Reformation truth. It was said of him: "If Knox as a young man had sneaked through trials the easiest way, he would never have had the strength in his prime to defy and rebuke [the queen]. It was by practicing the good habit of standing firm in small things against small people that Knox got the grace to stand firm in great things before great people."[3]

Every student of Christian history delights in the life of Charles Haddon Spurgeon. On April 17, 1887, Spurgeon preached a sermon from Philippians 4:1, in which he implored his listeners to stand firm in their doctrine, to stand firm in personal holiness, and to stand firm without wavering, wandering, or weariness.

Spurgeon thundered, "We must not yield, we dare not yield, if we are of the city of the great King. The martyrs cry to us to stand firm; the cloud of witnesses bending from their thrones above beseech us to stand firm; yes, all the hosts of the shining ones cry to us, 'Stand firm.' Stand firm for God, and the truth, and holiness, and let no man take your crown."

When Spurgeon saw his own denomination fall into theological erosion, he took a powerful stand. He stood firm at great personal cost, refusing to yield the high doctrines of the book he held in his hand.

Here in America, Jonathan Edwards ministered as the winds of the Enlightenment challenged the Christian message. But he never faltered, and his story is full of love, revival, and courage. In one of his incisive sermons, he said, "The servant who always stands watching will not be at all surprised at the news that his Lord is coming. This will be the way for you to live above the fear of death. Yea, if heaven and earth should shake, you may stand firm and unshaken, being settled on a rock, which cannot be removed, but abideth forever."[4]

In modern times, no one has influenced me more than Billy Graham, whom my wife and I had the opportunity of meeting on several occasions. He stood unflinchingly for the gospel. On one occasion he said,

> "Satan will do everything he can to divert us from the message of Scripture, but we must stand firm. God has spoken, and we must be faithful to that message. . . . Our generation, especially in the West, occupied itself with criticism of the Scriptures and all too soon found itself questioning divine revelation. Don't make that mistake. Take the Bible as God's holy Word. . . . I find that the Bible becomes a flame in my hands—a flame that melts the hearts of people and moves them to decide for Christ."[5]

I believe that Paul, too, was inspired by the Scriptures he studied, the hymns he sang, and the heroes he admired. In his writing he told us repeatedly to stand firm, rooted and grounded in Christ. Standing firm today—and doing so wisely, at the right times, without belligerence or hostility—is only possible for those who really study this concept in Scripture. It's not merely a human trait. It's only for those who are coached by the Scripture. Let me give you some critical passages about it.

Stand Firm in the Lord

In 1 Thessalonians 3:6–8, Paul wrote, "Timothy has just now come to us from you and has brought good news about your faith and love. . . . Therefore, brothers and sisters, in all our distress and persecution we were encouraged about you because of your faith. For now we really live, since you are standing firm in the Lord."

The apostle John wrote his first epistle because many people were defecting, leaving the faith. He told those who remained: "These people left our churches, but they never really belonged with us; otherwise they would have stayed with us. When they left, it proved that they did not belong with us. But you are not like that, for the Holy One has given you his Spirit, and all of you know the truth" (1 John 2:19–20 NLT).

We are not like the defectors, the deconstructionists, because we have the Holy Spirit and we know the truth, and that enables us to stand firm.

Stand Firm in the Liberty of Christ

Paul told the Galatians, "It is for freedom that Christ has set us free. Stand firm, then, and do not let yourselves be burdened again by a yoke of slavery" (Galatians 5:1). He didn't want anyone to dilute the teaching of the gospel.

Likewise, we must stand firm in our liberty. We must be free from anything that would enslave us, including the fear of men. Now more than ever, it's vital to hold unswervingly to the core doctrines of historic Christianity—the apostolic message—and to a biblical worldview on the burning issues of our day including the sanctity of sex, gender, and marriage. Our biblical worldview on these issues is wise, loving, and indispensable for the well-being of our culture. We must stand firm.

> WE ARE NOT LIKE THE DEFECTORS, THE DECONSTRUCTIONISTS, BECAUSE WE HAVE THE HOLY SPIRIT AND WE KNOW THE TRUTH, AND THAT ENABLES US TO STAND FIRM.

Stand Firm in the Faith

Paul told the Corinthians, "Be on your guard; stand firm in the faith; be courageous; be strong" (1 Corinthians 16:13). I have investigated Christianity from every angle, and I can tell you it is reliable and trustworthy, historically, philosophically, psychologically, prophetically, apologetically, archaeologically, scientifically, and in terms of its sublime humanitarianism that has changed human history. Someone told me once, "Doubt your doubts and believe your beliefs. Don't make the mistake of believing your doubts or doubting your beliefs."

Stand Firm, Clad in the Armor of God

In Ephesians 6:13–17, the Bible's premiere passage about spiritual warfare, we read:

Therefore put on the full armor of God, so that when the day of evil comes, you may be able to stand your ground, and after you have done everything, to stand. Stand firm then, with the belt of truth buckled around your waist, with the breastplate of righteousness in place, and with your feet fitted with the readiness that comes from the gospel of peace. In addition to all this, take up the shield of faith, with which you can extinguish all the flaming arrows of the evil one. Take the helmet of salvation and the sword of the Spirit, which is the word of God.

Stand Firm Against the Devil and His Schemes

Closely associated with that is Peter's command about Satan: "Resist him, standing firm in the faith, because you know that the family of believers throughout the world is undergoing the same kind of sufferings" (1 Peter 5:9).

Stand Firm in the Scriptures

Paul told the Thessalonians to stand firm in their doctrines, to the Scriptures, to the truths of God. He said, "So then, brothers and sisters, stand firm and hold fast to the teachings we passed on to you, whether by word of mouth or by letter" (2 Thessalonians 2:15).

This makes a titanic difference in our lives.

The American Bible Society released a report in 2023 based on data from nearly three thousand responses from adults in the United States. The study said, "Our research confirms something millions of Christians know through personal experience—that the Bible has the power to transform our lives and make us happier, healthier, and whole. We find that Christians who are committed to their faith, fully engaged in the Bible, and transformed by its message, flourish in every domain of human experience."

The report continued, "While these Scripture-engaged Christians go through the same hardships as everyone else, the difference is they experience life's ups and downs through a worldview shaped by the Bible's message of hope. No matter the circumstances, those who trust in God and connect with him through Scripture are happier than those who haven't yet sought God in His Word."[6]

Stand Firm in a Hostile World

All of this allows us to stand firm in a world that harbors an innate hostility toward Christianity. Proverbs 10:25 says, "When the storm has swept by, the wicked are gone, but the righteous stand firm forever."

Consider Lindsey Barr, for example. She was an assistant teacher with the Bryan County school system in Georgia. One day she learned that an inappropriate and sexually explicit book was going to be read to her three children in the library at McAllister Elementary School. This book also contained inappropriate drawings.

Lindsey asked the school principal to excuse her children from the reading program. In response the school fired her as a substitute teacher. Lindsey stood firm. Utilizing one of many groups that assist Christians who are being discriminated against in legal matters, she protested her firing. The Alliance Defending Freedom sent a letter to the school district asserting that her firing had violated her constitutional rights.

The school district had no choice but to agree. The school superintendent sent her a letter saying, "Upon returning, we encourage you as a parent to raise concerns about material being taught to your children. Raising such concerns does not preclude employment in our district. For the future, we are focused on the value you add for children across the district as a substitute teacher. We sincerely regret that your separation from the school district caused any distress."[7]

This kind of thing is being repeated again and again in our American story. We cannot always win, and we may face persecution and martyrdom. But whatever happens, we can stand firm.

In the village of Ano Vouves on the island of Crete is the oldest olive tree in the world. It's at least two thousand years old based on analysis, but it's likely much older. Scientists at the University of Crete believe it dates to the days of Abraham—four thousand years ago. It has withstood droughts and floods, storms and fires, bugs and blights. Its roots are firmly planted, and it still thrives. It still produces olives, and you can buy a bottle of its olive oil at a nearby gift shop.

Psalm 92 says that those who stand firm in their righteousness are like trees planted in the courtyards of the Lord. "They will still bear fruit in old age, they will stay fresh and green, proclaiming, 'The LORD is upright; he is my Rock, and there is no wickedness in him'" (vv. 14–15).

Notice the twin metaphors—tree and rock. When our roots infiltrate the deep, dark soil of Scripture, they embrace and interlace around a deeply buried unshakable rock, and the reason we don't blow over in the storms, the reason we can stand firm in all seasons is simple. Our roots are gripping the solid Rock. If you ever worry whether God can be pried loose from omnipotence, He cannot. If you're concerned He might forget even a preposition or period of one of His promises, He will not. When you think the storms are greater than the Stone to which you're anchored, they are not. Christ is greater than Gibraltar, greater than anything.

And with the writer of Psalm 61:2, you can say, "From the end of the earth I will cry to You. When my heart is overwhelmed; Lead me to the rock that is higher than I" (NKJV).

> **THE REASON WE CAN STAND FIRM IN ALL SEASONS IS SIMPLE. OUR ROOTS ARE GRIPPING THE SOLID ROCK.**

Do not be afraid. Stand firm and you will see the deliverance the LORD will bring you today.

EXODUS 14:13

You will not have to fight this battle. Take up your positions; stand firm and see the deliverance the LORD will give you, Judah and Jerusalem. Do not be afraid; do not be discouraged. Go out to face them tomorrow, and the LORD will be with you.

2 CHRONICLES 20:17

You will stand firm and without fear.

JOB 11:15

If you do not stand firm in your faith, you will not stand at all.

ISAIAH 7:9

You will be hated by everyone because of me, but the one who stands firm to the end will be saved.

MATTHEW 10:22

Stand firm, and you will win life.

LUKE 21:19

Therefore, my dear brothers and sisters, stand firm. Let nothing move you. Always give yourselves fully to the work of the Lord, because you know that your labor in the Lord is not in vain.

1 CORINTHIANS 15:58

Now it is God who makes both us and you stand firm in Christ.

2 CORINTHIANS 1:21

Chapter 24

WHATEVER HAPPENS . . .

HAVE A STRATEGY FOR IMPERFECT SITUATIONS

(PHILIPPIANS 4:2-7)

Years ago when our children were young and we were living in the church parsonage, Katrina worked all afternoon on her signature lasagna. She did everything from scratch, and when we peeked into the oven it was perfect—golden brown and hot and bubbling. She grabbed the potholders and, well, I still don't know what happened.

Somehow it slipped from her hands, flew through the air, and landed upside down on the kitchen floor. Katrina burst into tears. With the broom and dustpan and mop we disposed of it, as I tried to console Katrina. "It was the most perfect lasagna I'll never eat," I said.

We called in pizza.

Nothing is perfect in this life. Things get turned upside down all the time. Even a perfectly designed vacation will hit snags here and there. A perfect concert will have a discordant note somewhere, even if most people don't realize it. And how often have I told people, "There is no perfect church"?

The church in Philippi was about as perfect as we find in the New Testament, but there were a couple of women who had dropped the lasagna, as it were, and they were arguing about it. Paul wanted someone to console them and to send out for pizza. Philippians 4:2–3 says:

> I plead with Euodia and I plead with Syntyche to be of the same mind in the Lord. Yes, and I ask you, my true companion, help these women since they have contended at my side in the cause of the gospel, along with Clement and the rest of my co-workers, whose names are in the book of life.

Euodia and Syntyche were causing drama in the church, and Paul wanted the others to help them resolve it. I've been in situations like that. We all have—in our churches or homes or marriages or teams. Even if we're even-tempered and patient, we find our emotions starting to churn as we get drawn into the soap opera.

What can we do?

Beginning in verse 4, Paul gave us a list of actions for imperfect situations. We have a series of five statements that scholars call a paraenesis, a short set of instructions given in a staccato style. The apostle often did this at the end of his letters. He had more he wanted to say, but he was running out of parchment, so he used what we call today "bullet points." Look at verses 4–7:

> Rejoice in the Lord always. I will say it again: Rejoice! Let your gentleness be evident to all. The Lord is near. Do not be anxious about anything, but in every situation, by prayer and petition, with thanksgiving, present your requests to God. And the peace of God, which transcends all understanding, will guard your hearts and your minds in Christ Jesus.

Rejoice in the Lord Always

Paul revived his words from Philippians 3:1, suggesting we can handle imperfect situations better if we don't let them steal our joy. Paul was using Old

Testament language here. The phrase "rejoice in the Lord" occurs only in the Old Testament and in the book of Philippians. It seems Paul had been studying his books and parchments. He'd been impacted by this phrase, which was often used in the Old Testament by people facing difficult imperfections in their circumstances.

For example, the Old Testament hero Hannah was ensnarled in a very difficult domestic situation. She went to the tabernacle in Shiloh and prayed earnestly about it, and later she offered one of the most beautiful prayers in the Bible. It begins, "My heart rejoices in the LORD" (1 Samuel 2:1).

In Psalm 32, David faced the deep guilt of his sins and confessed them. He ended that prayer saying, "Rejoice in the LORD and be glad" (v. 11).

The most visual description of faith in the Bible is given at the end of Habakkuk: "Though the fig tree does not bud and there are no grapes on the vines, though the olive crop fails and the fields produce no food, though there are no sheep in the pen and no cattle in the stalls, yet I will rejoice in the LORD" (Habakkuk 3:17–18).

Here in the book of Philippians, the imprisoned apostle was writing to a somewhat divided church, advising them to rejoice in the Lord. When we can't rejoice in our load, our losses, our loneliness, or our lot in life, we can still rejoice in the Lord. We rejoice in His presence around us, His Word within us, His promises to us, His care over us, and His future for us.

WHEN WE CAN'T REJOICE IN OUR LOAD, OUR LOSSES, OUR LONELINESS, OR OUR LOT IN LIFE, WE CAN STILL REJOICE IN THE LORD.

I recall one day being depressed and anxious. I wanted the joy of God to fill my heart, but I was consumed with worry. Somehow the words came to me of this great hymn by Henry Van Dyke:

> *Joyful, joyful, we adore Thee,*
> *God of glory, Lord of love;*
> *Hearts unfold like flowers before Thee,*
> *Opening to the sun above.*
> *Melt the clouds of sin and sadness,*
> *Drive the dark of doubt away;*

> *Giver of immortal gladness,*
> *Fill us with the light of day.*[1]

That prayer became real to me, and I prayed it earnestly: *Lord, melt the clouds of sin and sadness. Drive the dark of doubt away. Giver of immortal gladness, fill me with the light of day.* The Lord answered that prayer, and in the years since, I feel I've been growing in the joy of the Lord. We simply have to make up our minds to do it: *Rejoice in the Lord always. I will say it again: Rejoice!*

Let Your Gentleness Be Evident to All

The next thing Paul told us is to be gentle (v. 5). This is a most convicting verse for me because, for much of my life, I didn't know how to be gentle. The biggest barriers to gentleness are our anger, our temper, our pride, and selfishness.

When I was starting as a writer, a magazine asked me to review a book and, if possible, interview the author. I read the book and liked it, but I found the author very difficult. He was rude. Having his name on the front of a book had gone to his head, and I came away as a young writer saying, "I never want to be like that person." Sometimes we learn from negative examples.

The Greek word for gentleness, *epieikes*, has to do with being gracious. It has to do with etiquette.

Gentleness doesn't mean a lack of strength or drive or determination. It means that your strength, drive, and determination are cloaked with graciousness.

In Luke 4:22, the people were amazed at the gracious words that came from our Lord's lips. And Colossians 4:6 (TLB) says, "Let your conversation be gracious as well as sensible, for then you will have the right answer for everyone."

This is most important in the home and family, with our husband or wife or children or in-laws, and then in the church and community. Things are not perfect in this world. Nothing about our lives is perfect. Nothing about our health, nothing about our finances, nothing about our homes or churches.

But harshness always makes things worse; gentleness makes things better.

Remember the Lord Is Near

The third item in this paraenesis is: "The Lord is near." Though simple, it's difficult to interpret. About half of the scholars believe Paul was talking in eschatological terms, saying that the Lord's return is near. Just a few verses before, at the end of chapter 3, Paul had told us to eagerly await the Savior from heaven who will transform our bodies to be like His glorified and glorious body.

The other half of the commentators believe Paul was referring to the geographical presence of Christ, that He is near us by the Holy Spirit. His presence is near. The book of James tells us to draw near to Him, and the psalmist said that the nearness of our God is our good.

I don't think we have to decide about it. Paul was using a literary device known as a *double entendre*. When we hear that term, we usually think of an innocent statement that hides a vulgar meaning. But the phrase simply means a statement that can be taken in two ways.

We certainly know both interpretations represent reality, don't we? The Lord's coming is near, and His presence is also near. Even when we don't feel the Lord's presence, He's still as near as ever. Sometimes, however, He gives us a keen sense of His nearness.

In the early years of Christian radio, the *Old Fashioned Revival Hour* was broadcast around the globe. A pilot was listening as he flew over Guam during the Second World War. He later wrote,

"Hearing the chorus singing, 'I would love to tell you what I think of Jesus,' was almost too much. As I remember it now, Bill MacDougall was singing a solo part, with the chorus in the background. When they all opened up on that chorus of the song, it seemed as if the sky had rolled back and we were standing at the very gates of heaven. Never in my life have I known the very nearness and presence of the Lord as I did at that moment."[2]

How wonderful to have moments like that. But regardless of our emotions, the Lord is near His every child. When your situation takes an imperfect turn, set your mind on the nearness of Christ.

Do Not Be Anxious About Anything

I tend to be anxious about everything. The only good thing about that is this: it has driven me to study everything the Bible has to say on the subject. The whole Bible is given to keep us from fear and worry. It's the greatest collection of antiworry advice in the world. I've found strength and reassurance on every page, but there are three passages that seem to me as definitive words from God on this subject. The first is Psalm 37, which begins, "Do not fret." The second is from the lips of our Lord in the Sermon on the Mount:

> Therefore I tell you, do not worry. . . . Look at the birds of the air; they do not sow or reap or store away in barns, and yet your heavenly Father feeds them. Are you not much more valuable than they? Can any one of you by worrying add a single hour to your life? And why do you worry about clothes? See how the flowers of the field grow. They do not labor or spin. . . . So do not worry . . . Seek first his kingdom and his righteousness, and all these things will be given to you as well. Therefore do not worry about tomorrow, for tomorrow will worry about itself. (Matthew 6:25–34)

The third passage is this one in Philippians 4:4–7. May I suggest that, if you battle worry, take the flyleaf of your Bible and write the words "Antiworry Verses." Then start with these three: Psalm 37, Matthew 6, and Philippians 4. When you find other verses that help you, write them down, too, and create your own list of antiworry passages.

Into your imperfect situation, God the Father says in the Old Testament: "Do not fret." God the Son says in the gospel: "Do not worry." And God the Holy Spirit inspired the words of Philippians 4:6: "Do not be anxious." Think of the three members of the Godhead hovering around you and speaking these words into your ears.

In Every Situation, By Prayer and Petition, With Thanksgiving, Present Your Requests to God

The final strategy for dealing with imperfection through prayer and thanksgiving is this: "In every situation, by prayer and petition, with thanksgiving, present your requests to God." Let me mention three things about this verse.

First, it involves an exchange. We're to trade in our problems for prayer. The Living Bible says, "Don't worry about anything; instead, pray about everything."

Second, it is comprehensive. Do not worry about *anything*, not one thing. Nothing. But pray about *everything*. Every single thing that bothers you. Notice those two words: *anything* and *everything*.

Third, don't forget to add thanksgiving to your prayers. This is master psychology. This is graduate-level information about the soul.

Dr. James Moore was a noted Methodist pastor in Houston. While traveling on a speaking engagement, he had occasion to eat supper with a young family. When they sat down at the table, the wife explained they'd been working on helping their children learn the importance of prayer and thanksgiving before meals. Each night, they asked one of the children to say the blessing.

As they bowed their heads, it was the little boy's turn to pray. He launched in and began to thank God for every dish on the table by name—the roast, the mashed potatoes, the corn, the rolls, and so on.

Then he gave thanks for all of the people present by name. This included his parents, siblings, their guest, Dr. Moore, and even their dog, Spot.

Finally, he moved on to all of the items in the home for which they should be grateful and again went into specifics by expressing gratitude for the table, the chairs, the silverware, the plates, and glasses, and on and on it went.

The siblings began to giggle. But when it was over, Dr. Moore admitted he was strangely moved. This four-year-old had reminded him of how important counting our blessings—all of our blessings—can be. How much God has given us, and how little of it do we thank Him for.

Dr. Moore was so moved, he later wrote a book about the importance of thanking God for even the simplest things in life.[3]

As we learn to do the five things in Philippians 4:4–7, God does something incredible for us. Verse 7 says He sends us His peace that exceeds human comprehension to guard our hearts and minds in Christ Jesus.

The peace of God is like a sentinel, like a ranger, like a Army Ranger that goes with you everywhere to protect your mind and your emotions from being attacked by Satan's weapon of worry.

No, nothing is perfect in this world.

But God has a strategy for imperfect times, and He gives His perfect peace to us—His imperfect people.

Chapter 25

WHATEVER HAPPENS . . .

IMPROVE YOUR MENTAL CHEMISTRY

(PHILIPPIANS 4:8–9)

Celebrity doctor Daniel Amen has extensively researched the brain. Some of his views are controversial, but I wanted to share a few intriguing sentences from one of his books.

- You are not stuck with the brain you have. You can make it better. . . . You can literally change your brain, and when you do, you change your life. . . . Learning to love and care for your brain will also decrease your stress, improve your relationships, increase your chances of success in every area of your life, help stave off dementia, and prevent you from becoming a burden to others.[1]
- [You can] master your brain by controlling what goes into it.[2]
- How you feel is often related to the quality of your thoughts.[3]
- Watching just fourteen consecutive minutes of negative news has been found to increase both anxious and sad moods.[4]

- Each thought you have triggers the release of certain chemicals, which makes you feel good or bad.[5]
- Direct your attention toward what you are grateful for, and your brain will work better.[6]

This is not exactly new advice. Look at Philippians 4:8–9:

Finally, brothers and sisters, whatever is true, whatever is noble, whatever is right, whatever is pure, whatever is lovely, whatever is admirable—if anything is excellent or praiseworthy—think about such things. Whatever you have learned or received or heard from me, or seen in me—put it into practice. And the God of peace will be with you.

The key imperative here is to "think about such things." The Lord is concerned with what goes on in our minds every day. What do we think about? What images or information are we depositing in our minds? What do we daydream about? What's our first thought in the morning and our last at night? What attitudes fill our minds?

Such Things

Theologian William Barclay wrote, "It is a law of life that if a [person] thinks of something often enough, he will come to the stage when he cannot stop thinking about it. His thoughts will be quite literally in a groove out of which he cannot jerk them."[7]

Just today a bad experience from the past was brought to my mind, and like a posttraumatic trigger, anger and confusion flooded my thoughts. I had to force my mind to quote Scripture and shift gears. We have to move from distressed thoughts to the blessed thoughts referred to here.

In this passage, Paul lists eight qualities that should rule our thought life.

Whatever is true. When I was thirteen or so, I was walking through my aunt Louise's factory. There was dangerous equipment there, but I could pass through safely if I followed a path that had been marked out by white lines. I was doing so when I saw two workers laughing about something. I got it into my mind they were laughing at me. I worried about what had caused them to laugh. Was it because I was pudgy? Was it because my face was broken out? Was it my clothes? Well, now I realize their laughter surely had nothing to do with me. I was letting a self-fabricated lie bounce around in my mind. How easily that still happens.

Whatever is noble. The Greek word for noble, *semnos*, means something awe-inspiring, majestic, and great. In the New Testament, it described things that were worthy of reverence. As I'm writing this chapter, strikes are breaking out in France and garbage trucks haven't been running. Tourists in Paris are walking down sidewalks lined with bags of garbage. That's not pleasant, but they can choose what they focus on. They can be obsessed with the garbage or they can lift their eyes above the streets and see the great monuments like the Arc de Triomphe, the Eiffel Tower, and the soaring windows in Sainte-Chapelle. Our thoughts can be in the gutter or we can rise above the gutter and think of noble things.

Whatever is right. The Greek word here is *dikaios*, often translated *righteous* in the Bible. The word "righteous" occurs forty-two times in Romans, more than in any other book of the New Testament. Romans 14:17 says, "For the kingdom of God is not a matter of eating and drinking, but of righteousness, peace and joy in the Holy Spirit." That's a great subject for a wandering mind.

Whatever is pure. This means something uncontaminated, like pure water or gold. In moral terms it means something that isn't tarnished or tainted with sinful images or impulses. I can't imagine having a totally pure heart like the one I'll have in heaven. But we should increasingly banish impure motives, images, sources of entertainment, words, and patterns of behavior. How? By focusing on purity. Paul told Timothy, "Keep yourself pure" (1 Timothy 5:22). How are you doing at that?

Whatever is lovely. This refers to something pleasing to see. It comes from the Greek word *phileo*, which means brotherly love. It's the joy of seeing a friend, a landscape, or a Bible verse we cherish. Recently I've seen a series of advertisements for Switzerland. I've visited that amazing nation several times, but the images in the advertisements exceeded my memories. What if you had in your heart the loveliness of Swiss oxygen and on your face the beauty of Swiss vigor?

A lovely personality comes from thinking about lovely things—including the person of God, the character of Christ, the wonder of worship, and the beauty of your beloved Bible verses.

Whatever is admirable. This is a straightforward term—something we can admire. Ask yourself who you most admire. Now ask who you most admire in the Old Testament. In the New Testament? In the history of the church? What personality traits do you most applaud? What biblical truths do you most cherish? Think more and more about these things. Learn to fall asleep with admirable thoughts of thanksgiving and gratitude.

Whatever is excellent. This means excellence of quality or character. The New Testament worker Titus was laboring on the island of Crete with people who were undisciplined and careless in their way of life. Paul gave him three chapters of instructions—our biblical book of Titus—and told him: "I want you to stress these things, so that those who have trusted in God may be careful to devote themselves to doing what is good. These things are excellent" (Titus 3:8).

Maybe we need to spend a bit more time in Titus.

Whatever is praiseworthy. This refers to something you can applaud. I once heard the president of the United States speak in a high school gymnasium. I liked some of the things he said and applauded them. He said other things I strongly disagreed with, and I didn't applaud those statements. We need to fill our minds with thoughts that God applauds.

Think

Now we come to that primary verb, *think*. How practical. How applicable. Instead of letting our feelings run wild, we have to stop ourselves, remind ourselves, and train ourselves to think. What do you think about upon awakening? In the shower? As you drive to work or school?

Or do we think at all? Do we simply yield to the earbud phenomenon?

The twenty-four-hour news cycle? The endless gaming and video options that virtually hypnotize the mind?

I have to take walks to think, float in the pool to think, turn off the car radio to think, and remind myself to list three items of thanksgiving about the day before falling asleep.

Going through life, we're confronted with much that has the opposite qualities from Philippians 4. I grew up with newspapers coming to my house every day, and I still get three daily newspapers, though they now come to my tablet. Every morning I spend a few minutes catching up on the nation and the world, thinking about warfare, death, and destruction. I think about political polarization. I read about the persecution of Christians, about secularity, and about all manner of evil bedeviling the planet.

Are we not to think about those things?

Well, we're to be aware of them and understand the times. But the word *think* is translated differently in other Bible versions.

- The New King James Version says "meditate on these things."
- The Christian Standard Bible says "dwell on these things."
- The New American Standard Bible 1995 says "dwell on these things."
- The Contemporary English Version says "keep your minds on [these things]."
- The Amplified Bible says "think continually on these things [center your mind on them, and implant them in your heart]."
- The Good News Translation says "fill your minds [with these things]."

There are some things we should never let into our minds—books, images, and websites to avoid at all costs. There are other things like social trends and world events we should be aware of, but when it comes to allowing our minds to dwell on things and to meditate, Paul was simply reminding us what the entire Bible teaches about guarding our minds.

- "Blessed is the one . . . whose delight is in the law of the LORD, and who meditates on his law day and night." (Psalm 1:1–2)

- "You will keep in perfect peace those whose minds are steadfast, because they trust in you." (Isaiah 26:3)
- "Those who live according to the flesh have their minds set on what the flesh desires; but those who live in accordance with the Spirit have their minds set on what the Spirit desires. The mind governed by the flesh is death, but the mind governed by the Spirit is life and peace." (Romans 8:5–6)
- "Set your minds on things above, not on earthly things." (Colossians 3:2)

Biblical Worldview

How Do We Do This?

When it comes to biblical and Godward meditation, I have four steps to suggest: read the Bible; remember what you've read; ruminate on it; and realign yourself to Scripture.

First, we have to read our Bibles. This wasn't always true, because many periods of history were illiterate. People didn't know how to read, and in some cases, they didn't even have a written language. Others had a written language but no easy way to produce literature. Instead they would hear and learn vast portions of material orally. But today global literacy stands at 87 percent, and in most developed countries that number is 99 percent.

We praise God for that, because it gives us the opportunity of having a personal copy of God's Word that we can read for ourselves. The Lord expects us to read the Bible. It bothered Jesus greatly when His audiences didn't read and ponder the Scriptures. Look at His "haven't you read" statements in Matthew's gospel:

- "Haven't you read what David did when he and his companions were hungry?" (Matthew 12:3)
- "Or haven't you read in the Law that the priests on Sabbath duty in the temple desecrate the Sabbath and yet are innocent?" (Matthew 12:5)
- "Haven't you read . . . that at the beginning the Creator 'made them male and female.'" (Matthew 19:4)

- "Have you never read, 'From the lips of children and infants you, Lord, have called forth your praise'?" (Matthew 21:16)
- "Have you never read in the Scriptures: 'The stone the builders rejected has become the cornerstone'?" (Matthew 21:42)
- "But about the resurrection of the dead—have you not read what God said to you?" (Matthew 22:31)

The Lord expects us to read the book He's given us.

Something happens when we begin reading the Bible seriously every day. In her blog *Then She Spoke,* Annette Coffey writes about how she had a massive stroke at age forty-five and was unable to speak for seven years. Even now, she has trouble pronouncing some words, so she writes more than she talks. In a blog entry, she wrote:

> I believe now that my stroke was the most important thing that ever happened to me. . . . I have come to not only believe in my God but got to know Him and His character so very well that I realize that I can't possibly live a minute without him. Nor do I ever want to. I began reading the Bible every day the year after my stroke. And though at times it has been tough, I committed to read straight through from the beginning to the end. The only way you can have a real good relationship with someone is to get to know everything that is important to them and by sharing everything that is important to you also. That's why reading the Bible and prayer is so valuable. It's actually better than the best textbook, owner's manual, or guidebook for life, and it was inspired by the very one who made us and knows what is best for us. . . . I can honestly say that I have never been more at peace, happier, more fulfilled than I am right now.[8]

You don't necessarily have to read from Genesis to Revelation, but I suggest reading today where you left off yesterday. I like to read the Bible with a pen or pencil in my hand, making notes and underscoring verses that really speak to me.

You can do this. You can read your Bible every day. Even a child can do this—and should. Even a teenager can do this—and should. Find an easy-to-read translation and get started today.

Second, remember what you've read. Vera Schmitz was an athlete from Missouri, an Olympic hopeful and All-American pole vaulter. Whenever she competed, she would write a Scripture verse with a Sharpie on her arm. Later she started a website to help people memorize Scripture. She suggests aids such as Scripture cards, key chains, and even temporary tattoos to help remember verses we're working on.

I go to antique stores and look for framed Scripture verses in watercolor, cross-stitching, or calligraphy. I often give these to friends. Deuteronomy 6 says we should post Bible verses on the walls of our houses. We should surround ourselves with reminders of God's Word.

Devise your own ways of remembering and memorizing key verses the Lord gives you.

> DEVISE YOUR OWN WAYS OF REMEMBERING AND MEMORIZING KEY VERSES THE LORD GIVES YOU.

Third, ruminate on what you've read. I could have used the word "reflect," but as I prepared this chapter, I read a book entitled *The Art of Divine Meditation* by Edmund Calamy, a London Puritan. He referenced a most unlikely passage to demonstrate his point about meditation. Leviticus 11 says there are clean and unclean animals. Animals that chew the cud are clean; the ones that don't are not.

Calamy said the same is true for people. The ones who chew the cud are clean and getting cleaner every day. What did he mean by that?

Some barnyard animals like cows and sheep have a divided stomach. They graze and eat all they can, swallowing it whole. Later they find a shady spot, regurgitate that food, and chew it thoroughly before swallowing it again. This special stomach is called the rumen, and that's where we get our word *ruminate*. It means letting our minds chew on what we've read and remembered.

Calamy wrote: "A meditating Christian is one that chews the cud, that chews on the truths of Jesus Christ, that does not only hear good things, but when he has heard them, chews them over, ruminates on them, so that they may be more fit for digestion and concoction, and spiritual improvement."[9]

Say you're focusing your attention on this particular verse—Philippians

4:8. As you sit in the backyard, put down your phone and just think about this verse. Consider what's been occupying your mind. Has it been filled with worry? With impure images? With nonstop coverage of the news? Are those things excellent or praiseworthy?

Sit there and ruminate about this. In fact, pause your reading a moment and deliberately think about Philippians 4:8. Quote it to yourself. Measure yourself by its superb terms.

When preparing sermons, I find that after I've studied the selected passage, I inevitably have to take a walk or pace back and forth, trying to figure out how to explain it and make it practical to life.

That is rumination. That is reflection. It's biblical meditation. When we ruminate on Scripture, we let it change our thoughts, change our attitudes, and change our behavior.

Finally, we realign. We read, remember, ruminate, and then we realign our life to what we've learned. We respond. We are transformed by the renewing of our minds.

The Bible promises that the God of peace will be with us during the process. It is through this process that we claim the promise that the God of peace will be with us.

The *Washington Post* recently ran an article entitled "America Was Obsessed with this Self-Help Craze 100 Years Ago." During the Roaring Twenties, a Frenchman named Émile Coué developed a concept called autosuggestion. This fad swept over America, and everyone was caught up in it. Here's what people did:

They bought a strand of twenty beads, and every morning when they woke up, sometimes without even getting out of bed, they repeated twenty times in succession: "Day by day, in every way, I am getting better and better."

They could keep count of how many times they said it by moving their fingers through the beads, one at a time, like using a rosary. In the evening when going to bed, they'd do the same.

For a while, Coué was the most talked-about man in the country. He died in 1926, and Americans quickly forgot the frenzy, but his ideas lived on. The *Post* said he paved the way for the likes of Dale Carnegie, Norman Vincent

Peale, and more recently Oprah Winfrey, who told her followers: "Look at yourself in a full-length mirror. Now compliment yourself. Yes, you can do it. Repeat those empowering words aloud every morning and every night."[10]

I'm not selling any beads or pushing any self-help slogans. But when it comes to the specific Bible verses God gives you, I want to suggest repeating them over and over, finding ways to read, remember, ruminate, and respond.

In closing, let me give you what I imagine the devil's version of Philippians 4:8 to be:

> Finally, my pushovers, whatever is disturbing, whatever is worrisome, whatever is sleazy, whatever is impure, whatever is worthless, whatever is filthy, whatever is doubtful, whatever is bitter—if there is anything crude and perishable—think on these things, and the heartaches of the world will engulf you.

You and I must choose which "translation" we'll use every moment of every day. Our thoughts take on a life of their own, forming our personalities and crystalizing them like, well, either like a piece of gravel or a gem. You can listen to the devil's adaptation if you want. But for what it's worth, I suggest the original version.

Chapter 26

WHATEVER HAPPENS . . .

DISCOVER THE SECRET
TO CONTENTMENT

(PHILIPPIANS 4:10-13)

I enjoy visiting Washington, DC, and the city's museums, the Smithsonian, the National Gallery, and my favorite—the Museum of the Bible. But there's one museum I want to see more than any, and I can't get in. It's the secret museum of the Central Intelligence Agency, located at CIA headquarters in Langley, Virginia. The museum occupies eleven thousand square feet and reportedly contains all kinds of spy gadgets, espionage memorabilia, and unusual weapons.

Only employees of the CIA are admitted.

Washington is a city of top secrets and classified information. I hope the government will soon declassify all the files related to the assassination of President Kennedy—which I remember—so we'll finally know what actually happened to the man.

The Lord has secrets, too, and sometimes He declassifies some of them for us. That brings us to the next paragraph in Philippians 4, verses 10–13:

I rejoiced greatly in the Lord that at last you renewed your concern for me. Indeed, you were concerned, but you had no opportunity to show it. I am not saying this because I am in need, for I have learned to be content whatever the circumstances. I know what it is to be in need, and I know what it is to have plenty. I have learned the secret of being content in any and every situation, whether well fed or hungry, whether living in plenty or in want. I can do all this through him who gives me strength.

God Has Secrets

Paul had learned one of God's secrets. It's interesting to think in these terms. Look, for example, at Deuteronomy 29. In this chapter, Moses was very old and nearing the time of his death. He gathered the nation of Israel and led them to renew their commitment to God. He explained what the Lord would do for them if they remained true to Him, and what the Lord would do if they forsook Him. Moses implored them to obey the law they had been given.

The final verse, Deuteronomy 29:29, says, "The secret things belong to the LORD our God, but the things revealed belong to us and to our children forever, that we may follow all the words of this law."

God has declassified a great deal of information. He has given us sixty-six books of the Bible, plus the entire physical universe as a classroom. But there are things He has not told us. After all, He is omniscient. Isaiah 55:8–9 says, "My thoughts are not your thoughts . . . . As the heavens are higher than the earth, so are . . . my thoughts [higher] than your thoughts."

But God does reveal some secrets. Isaiah 45:3 says, "I will give you hidden treasures, riches stored in secret places, so that you may know that I am the LORD, the God of Israel, who summons you by name."

This was originally addressed to King Cyrus as a prophetic statement by Isaiah, but there's application here for us too. God gives us the hidden treasures of His secrets.

When Jesus came, He revealed more secrets, helping us to formulate a clearer picture of the gospel. He told His disciples, "The knowledge of the secrets of the kingdom of heaven has been given to you" (Matthew 13:11).

When it comes to God's secrets, however, there's one thing that even Jesus in His humanity did not know—the exact time of His second coming. "About that day or hour," Jesus said, "no one knows, not even the angels in heaven, nor the Son, but only the Father" (Matthew 24:36).

God had another secret the apostle Paul learned over time. Philippians 4:10 says, "I rejoiced greatly in the Lord that at last you renewed your concern for me. Indeed, you were concerned, but you had no opportunity to show it."

Remember that the Philippians had been Paul's best supporting church, sending him needed funds again and again. This time they had sent money by the hand of Epaphroditus, and Paul was thanking them.

He went on to write in verse 11: "I am not saying this because I am in need, for I have learned to be content whatever the circumstances."

Notice the simple statement: "I have learned to be content." He explained further in verse 12: "I know what it is to be in need, and I know what it is to have plenty."

Some days Paul stayed in the wealthy villas of friends and was cared for by wealthy Christians; other times he was exposed to the weather or having to scramble for food. But he was as content in one situation as in the other.

Verse 12 finishes with: "I have learned the secret of being content in any and every situation, whether well fed or hungry, whether living in plenty or in want."

The Greek word Paul used here is amazing. It's a Greek technical term. If you read this phrase in English, it is made up of five words: "I have learned the secret." But in the Greek, the entire phrase is one short word: *memyemai*.

This is the only time this word occurs in the Bible. It means to be initiated into mysteries. In secular Greek usage, it had to do with the mysteries of the magical cults. To become a candidate for a mystery religion, you had to go through various kinds of initiations or rituals. After you learned the mysteries, you had to take a vow of silence.

In the second temple period, this term was sometimes used to describe the top secret information a king issued involving a war or a matter of national security.

Paul said, "I have learned something top secret—classified information." He had uncovered one of God's best secrets.

One of His Secrets Has to Do with Contentment

Paul said, "I have learned to be content. . . . I have learned the secret of being content."

This is a very hard thing for us to learn. At some level, if we were truly contented, we would be just as satisfied in our hearts whether we were in a hospital bed or at home. In a one-room apartment or a three-bedroom house. Being single or being married. Staying in a 1950s-era motel or the Waldorf Astoria. We wouldn't care if we were in coach or first class. Being successful would mean nothing more than failure and defeat. Whether we won or lost the game, either would be fine. Wow.

I'm not there yet. I'm not always content when things aren't as I want them to be. I have to really work on it. But in order to get there, we have to know exactly what contentment is. I've worked and worked on a definition of contentment—and my best suggestion is *quiet joy*.

Contentment isn't loud joy. It's not shouting in exuberance; it's not like the finale of a fireworks show. It is quiet joy, like the sound of a gentle rain or the purring of a cat. It's the green pastures and still waters of Psalm 23. It's the glow of a campfire or the sound of leaves crunching under our feet in the fall. It's a hot cup of tea, sweetened with honey and good to the last drop. It's lighting a candle on an overcast day or grabbing an extra blanket on a cold night.

Contentment is the quiet joy of knowing the eternal God is our refuge and underneath are the everlasting arms. We may not have everything we want or even need, but we have *Him*—and that gives us the inward, quiet joy that we call contentment.

Few people have written about this except for a couple of great Puritan writers long ago. But one man did. Pastor Erik Raymond wrote a book called

Chasing Contentment, which he defined this way: "Contentment is the inward, gracious, quiet spirit that joyfully rests in God's providence."[1]

The Bible devotes several verses to this:

- I have calmed and quieted myself, I am like a weaned child with its mother; like a weaned child I am content. (Psalm 131:2)
- But godliness with contentment is great gain. For we brought nothing into the world, and we can take nothing out of it. But if we have food and clothing, we will be content with that. (1 Timothy 6:6–8)
- Keep your lives free from the love of money and be content with what you have, because God has said, "Never will I leave you; never will I forsake you." (Hebrews 13:5)

Notice Paul didn't say he had learned contentment. He said he had learned the *secret* to contentment. Contentment is one of the Lord's secrets. Somehow Paul uncovered it. The Lord has a secret code that unlocks contentment, and Paul discovered it over time.

What was it?

I know what it is, and I'm not going to sell it to you. I'll give it to you for free, absolutely without charge. God's secret code to discovering and learning to be content are the numbers 413.

Philippians 4:13.

And the Secret to Contentment Is . . .

Philippians 4:13 says, "I can do all this through him who gives me strength." Let's look at this from several translations so we can get the force of it.

- I have the strength to face all conditions by the power that Christ gives me. (Good News Translation)
- I am ready for anything through the strength of the one who lives within me. (J. B. Phillips)

- I can be content in any and every situation through the Anointed One who is my power and strength. (The Voice)
- I have strength for all things in Christ Who empowers me [I am ready for anything and equal to anything through Him Who infuses inner strength into me; I am self-sufficient in Christ's sufficiency]. (AMPC)

Philippians 4:13 is not an absolute promise that you can do anything you want to. God is not promising you'll run a four-minute mile or make a million dollars or hike the Appalachian Trail from Georgia to Mount Katahdin in Maine in one season. Perhaps He'll help you do one or all of those things, but this verse has the exact opposite meaning. It means that whether you reach your goal or ambition or not, He will give you the strength to have His quiet joy.

Many Christian athletes write Philippians 4:13 on their arms or on their sneakers—it's a good thing, but it doesn't mean God will give you the strength to win every event. Rather, He will give you strength to do your best and then handle the outcome with an inner peace and satisfaction, whatever happens.

In Christ we have everything we need. He infuses us with the strength we need to live contentedly, because we know, whatever the circumstances, He is with us; we know He is working, and that He has a wonderful, everlasting eternity ahead of us.

HE WILL GIVE YOU THE STRENGTH TO HAVE HIS QUIET JOY.

The secret, in other words, is Jesus Himself. It's the strength He brings to our hearts when He enters any situation with us. Being content depends on your content. It depends on having Jesus Christ within you by His Holy Spirit.

Recently I've circled back to an old gospel song about guidance. I've needed to know what to do about having a church to attend and a congregation to join. It's been traumatic for me to work through this issue because as an adult, I've always been a pastor. But recently, the Lord directed my attention back to the great song, "He Leadeth Me." One of the verses sums all this up with these words:

Lord, I would clasp thy hand in mine,
Nor ever murmur nor repine;
Content, whatever lot I see;

Since 'tis my God that leadeth me.
He leadeth me, he leadeth me;
By his own hand, he leadeth me.
His faithful follower I would be,
For by his hand he leadeth me.[2]

Let's be content whatever lot we see. Learn the secret of the great apostle who said: "I know what it is to be in need, and I know what it is to have plenty. I have learned the secret of being content in any and every situation, whether well fed or hungry, whether living in plenty or in want. I can do all this through him who gives me strength" (Philippians 4:12–13).

Chapter 27

WHATEVER HAPPENS . . .

TRUST GOD WITH EVERY SINGLE NEED

(PHILIPPIANS 4:14-20)

The other day a name popped up in the news I didn't know. Bernard Arnault is reportedly the single richest person on the entire planet. He's a Frenchman, a fashion industry executive who oversees the likes of Louis Vuitton, Christian Dior, Givenchy, Tiffany & Co., Marc Jacobs, Sephora, and many more. I wondered where such a person lives, so I searched online and found pictures of his expansive château in France. But there's also a penthouse in Paris, a vacation home in San Tropez, another vacation home in the Alps, an entire island in the Bahamas, five mansions in Los Angeles, and a very expensive home in the Hamptons. He also has jets and yachts. I expect he doesn't live in all those places; they're just part of his investment portfolio.

He is said to be worth $190.3 billion.[1]

But for all that, he is not as rich as the humblest child of God, and I'm not just speaking metaphorically. Look at Philippians 4:14–20:

Yet it was good of you to share in my troubles. Moreover, as you Philippians know, in the early days of your acquaintance with the gospel, when I set out from Macedonia, not one church shared with me in the matter of giving and receiving, except you only; for even when I was in Thessalonica, you sent me aid more than once when I was in need. Not that I desire your gifts; what I desire is that more be credited to your account. I have received full payment and have more than enough. I am amply supplied, now that I have received from Epaphroditus the gifts you sent. They are a fragrant offering, an acceptable sacrifice, pleasing to God. And my God will meet all your needs according to the riches of his glory in Christ Jesus. To our God and Father be glory forever and ever. Amen.

As we've seen, the church in Philippi is the New Testament's premier model of stewardship. In 2 Corinthians 8 and 9, Paul gave an extended talk about this. Now here at the end of Philippians, he circled back and thanked them again for the financial support they sent him while he was under house arrest in Rome. As we saw, Epaphroditus had been commissioned to travel the eight hundred or so miles and take their gift to Paul in Rome. That really was an extraordinary thing for a church to do.

As I noted earlier in this book, Dr. Matthew Harmon says the distance traveled could have ranged from seven hundred to twelve hundred miles, depending on the route taken and the time of year. The best estimates for the length of the trip by foot would be six weeks. But in less favorable circumstances, it would take three months.[2]

Epaphroditus became deathly ill after arriving in Rome, and Paul nursed him back to health. The apostle then penned this letter to the Philippians as a thank-you note, gave it to Epaphroditus, and sent him home. Here near the end of his remarks, Paul had said most of what he wanted to say. He brought the letter to its conclusion by formally thanking them and talking about the gift they sent.

The Final Paragraph in Philippians

Verse 14 says, "It was good of you to share in my troubles." In other words, Paul appreciated their partnering with him during his difficult time as a prisoner in Rome. In the same way, God blesses us when we're allowed to share in the troubles of others.

Verses 15 and 16 continue: "Moreover, as you Philippians know, in the early days of your acquaintance with the gospel, when I set out from Macedonia, not one church shared with me in the matter of giving and receiving, except you only; for even when I was in Thessalonica, you sent me aid more than once when I was in need."

Here Paul was thinking back over the years to the way the Philippians had sent him financial support. I can't imagine what this means to a missionary. Throughout my life, I've been fortunate to receive a paycheck for services rendered, first at places like JCPenney and Sears, and then at the churches I've pastored. But I've never had to raise my own support the way many missionaries must do. After watching this process for many decades, I can tell you it is harder for some missionaries than others. But I've grown in my conviction that a local church should as much as possible sponsor and support the missionaries it sends out. This is what the Philippians did for Paul. They became, in effect, his primary supporting church.

GOD BLESSES US WHEN WE'RE ALLOWED TO SHARE IN THE TROUBLES OF OTHERS.

Here at the end of the letter, then, he officially expressed his deepest gratitude. He went on to say in verse 17: "Not that I desire your gifts; what I desire is that more be credited to your account."

Paul may have been thinking of what Jesus said in Matthew 6:19–20: "Do not store up for yourselves treasures on earth, where moths and vermin destroy, and where thieves break in and steal. But store up for yourselves treasures in heaven."

In some sense, our financial support for the Lord's work on earth is credited to our account in heaven. Paul went on to use several other phrases to describe their gift. Look at verse 18: "I have received full payment and have more than enough.

I am amply supplied, now that I have received from Epaphroditus the gifts you sent. They are a fragrant offering, an acceptable sacrifice, pleasing to God."

The Final Promise in Philippians

And now we come to the glorious closing note of the book of Philippians: "And my God will meet all your needs according to the riches of his glory in Christ Jesus. To our God and Father be glory for ever and ever. Amen."

Dr. Gordon Fee wrote:

This sentence is a master stroke. Although [Paul] cannot reciprocate in kind, since their gift had the effect of being a sweet-smelling sacrifice, pleasing to God, Paul assures them that God, whom he deliberately designates as "my God," will assume responsibility for reciprocity. Thus, picking up the language of "my need" from verse 16 and "fill to the full" from verse 18, he promises them that "my God will fill up every need of yours."

In their present suffering in the face of opposition, God will richly supply what is needed (steadfastness, joy, encouragement). In their need to advance in the faith in one mindset, God will richly supply the grace and humility necessary for it. In the place of both "grumbling" and "anxiety," God will be present with them as the God of peace. "My God," Paul says, will act for me in your behalf by "filling to the full all your needs."[3]

This verse is simply a continuation of a theme we find throughout the Bible. When we put the Lord first in our lives—with our habits, our priorities, our giving, our living—He will make sure all our needs are met, whether those needs are financial, emotional, spiritual, relational, or whatever.

WHEN WE PUT THE LORD FIRST IN OUR LIVES, HE WILL MAKE SURE ALL OUR NEEDS ARE MET.

Psalm 23:1 says, "Because the Lord is my Shepherd, I have everything I need!" (TLB).

Matthew 6:33 says, "Seek ye first the kingdom of God . . . and all these things shall be added unto you" (KJV).

John 1:16 says, "From his abundance we have all received one gracious blessing after another" (NLT).

Philippians 4:19 says, "And my God shall supply all your need according to His riches in glory by Christ Jesus" (NKJV).

I graduated from Columbia International University in South Carolina, and for a time the president of that school was Dr. Mark Smith, whom we all loved and respected. Because of health issues, however, he had to step aside. But Dr. Smith told of a time when he and his wife, Debbie, were newly married, trying to graduate from college, and living on a shoestring. Tax season came, and they owed $278 in taxes. That doesn't seem like a lot to most of us now, but it was a whopping amount to that couple. They were so distressed that for thirty days they committed to fast from certain meals and to pray fervently for that money—$278.

Dr. Smith later said, "We claimed Philippians 4:19 as a promise that applied to our situation. . . . Paul wrote this promise to a church that had been giving sacrificially to his own ministry. And our finances were tight because we had followed God's guidance to attend Bible college."

Meanwhile, the youth group back at Mark's home church decided to take up an offering for them, and it amounted to $153. Mark's grandmother decided to send them a check for $100, and when her husband heard about it, he added another $25.

Mark and Debbie received the $278 in the mail down to the last cent. It was a lesson they never forgot.[4]

A woman wrote to the advice columnist of *Slate* magazine, saying, "My husband grew up poor in a single-parent household. I grew up better off. My parents were both good at saving, and good at investing money wisely. My husband knows we were better off, but I don't think he realizes just *how* well off. I'm wondering if I should prepare him in some way for when my mom passes away or just go the 'Surprise. We get a third of a multimillion dollar estate' route."[5]

We don't have any idea how rich we are and how wealthy we'll be in eternity because of the riches of God's grace gained by the death of Christ, but great comfort comes to those who learn Philippians 4:19: "And my God will meet all your needs according to the riches of his glory in Christ Jesus."

You can trust God to meet every single need in your life when He is first and foremost in your heart.

In the next two chapters, I would like to open the vault and show you twenty-four bottomless treasure chests that have your name on them.

Whatever happens, I don't want you to forget how rich you are.

Chapter 28

WHATEVER HAPPENS . . .

CONSIDER YOURSELF
WORTH MILLIONS PART 1

(PHILIPPIANS 4:19)

Some of the richest people on earth are the poorest—and, again, I'm not just speaking metaphorically. In 1975, on the day he turned twenty-one, John Hervey, 7th Marquess of Bristol, inherited a fortune that would equal $65 million today. At first, he increased his worth by wise investments and real estate deals. But he also bought yachts, sports cars, and escorts. He was handsome, charming, and known for his flamboyant lifestyle and sexual escapades. His growing drug habit became uncontrollable and sucked up millions of his dollars. He ended up depressed and penniless, dying from organ failure at age forty-four.[1]

Would you call him rich? Would God?

On the other hand, some of the poorest people on earth are the richest.

They are children of the King, and the Bible is something of a register of our riches. Let's go into the vault of Scripture, open the ledgers, and begin an impossible task—trying to calculate our wealth. In this chapter and the next are twenty-four Bible verses you should know.

Let's start with our key verse from Philippians:

PHILIPPIANS 4:19

According to the riches of his glory in Christ Jesus.

As we saw in the last chapter, Paul commended the Philippians for their support of global missions and the ongoing work of the church. He promised them they wouldn't lose by giving. Instead, he said, "My God will meet all your needs according to the riches of his glory in Christ Jesus." Our Lord possesses infinite wealth. His property extends to the edges of the universe and beyond. Psalm 50:10–12 says, "Every animal of the forest is mine, and the cattle on a thousand hills. I know every bird in the mountains, and the insects in the fields are mine. . . . The world is mine, and all that is in it."

The Lord's resources are infinite; His budget is limitless; His wealth is overflowing. He can certainly meet every need in your life according to the riches of His glory in Christ Jesus.

In all my biblical studies through the years, I have never seen such a list as this. I'm giving it to you in brief form but suggesting you find a time to go through these verses during your daily devotions, dwelling on them, relishing them, memorizing those that are most meaningful to you, and then sharing them with others. This list also provides excellent fodder for a group Bible study. I hope you enjoy it as much as I have enjoyed putting it together.

THE LORD'S RESOURCES ARE INFINITE; HIS BUDGET IS LIMITLESS; HIS WEALTH IS OVERFLOWING.

GENESIS 27:28

May God give you heaven's dew and earth's richness—
an abundance of grain and new wine.

In Genesis 27, Isaac blessed his son Jacob, asking God to meet his needs from earth's riches. When God created the world, He built into it all we need for life and prosperity. There's air to breathe; food to eat; sunshine to warm; sunsets to thrill us; sunrises to give us fresh starts; gravity to hold us down; aerodynamics to lift us up; soil to cultivate; gold to excavate; and water to quench our thirst.

EPHESIANS 1:7

In him we have redemption through his blood, the forgiveness
of sins, in accordance with the riches of God's grace.

The provisions of our privileged planet, however, can't meet the needs of
our souls. But the same God who built the provision of earth's richness for our
use and delight is also rich in grace. He is rich in love, and it touches you and
me in the vital center of our souls. (If you want a biblical study of our riches in
one extended passage, read the first three chapters of Ephesians.)

EPHESIANS 2:6–7

God raised us up with Christ . . . in order that in the coming
ages he might show the incomparable riches of his grace,
expressed in his kindness to us in Christ Jesus.

As rich as we are now, nothing can prepare us for the riches ahead of us—
the new heaven and the new earth, described in Revelation 21–22, with the
glorious capital city of New Jerusalem. That city is described for us so vividly
that we can visualize it—an enormous diamond city with streets that glisten
with gold, buildings effervescent with light, walls made of jewels, and gates
made of pearls. Mansions, status, purpose, activity, access to the eternal throne,
and undying worship.

2 CORINTHIANS 8:9

For you know the grace of our Lord Jesus Christ, that
though he was rich, yet for your sake he became poor, so
that you through his poverty might become rich.

Consider how the Son of God left the riches of His eternal empire to
become a penniless peasant, not having house or land, bed or pillow. He said,
"Foxes have dens and birds have nests, but the Son of Man has no place to lay
his head" (Matthew 8:20). Spurgeon said:

If our riches are really in proportion to His poverty, that poverty, even to bloody sweat and death upon the cross, was so extreme that our riches must be extreme, too. Lift up your eyes, ye sons of light, look beyond that narrow stream of death—over there is your heritage. Do you see that fair city smiling in everlasting light far brighter than the sun? Behold its jeweled courses and its twelve foundations, sparkling like a rainbow with diverse hues of wealth; and do you hear, as you stand outside its gates of pearl, the matchless melody of the new song that goes up day without night? Do you see the white robes of the shining ones, in peerless bliss, as they traverse the pavements of gold, and cast their crowns at the feet of the King their Lord and Savior? All that is yours, and your Lord has given you a guarantee that you shall have it, and all that is needed to bring you there in due time.[2]

LUKE 12:21 AND 1 TIMOTHY 6:18

This is how it will be with whoever stores up things
for themselves but is not rich toward God.

Command them to do good, to be rich in good deeds,
and to be generous and willing to share.

The first quote is from Jesus' story of the rich man and Lazarus. In describing the rich man in the misery of his afterlife, Jesus said he was not rich toward God in this life. In 1 Timothy, the Lord tells us it's possible to be rich in good deeds. If, for the moment, we are not rich in money, land, and assets, we can certainly be rich toward God and rich in good deeds.

JAMES 2:5

Listen, my dear brothers and sisters: Has not God chosen those
who are poor in the eyes of the world to be rich in faith and
to inherit the kingdom he promised those who love him?

We can also be rich in faith, prospecting out and claiming all of the rich promises of God in the Bible and focusing our attention on them in times of difficulty.

RUTH 2:12

May the LORD repay you for what you have done. May you
be richly rewarded by the LORD, the God of Israel, under
whose wings you have come to take refuge.

These words were spoken by Boaz to Ruth, who had left everything to seek the God of Israel, alongside her mother-in-law Naomi. God opened the heart of Boaz, and he bestowed this blessing on her. It came true in spades. Ruth became his wife, the great-grandmother of King David, a woman whose name is in the lineage of Christ, and the hero of a love story for the ages. The Lord does indeed richly reward those who seek refuge under his wings.

PSALM 119:14

I rejoice in following your statutes as one rejoices in great riches.

What if you had thirty-one thousand checks, each made out for one million dollars? We have more than thirty-one thousand verses in the Bible, each of them of infinite worth. Every one represents a precious word God has sent down from heaven for our guidance, our good, and our godliness. We should enjoy opening our Bibles every day as much as we enjoy whatever money comes our way. It's like cashing a large check every day. Psalm 19 says that the words of Scripture are "more precious than gold, than much pure gold. . . . By them your servant is warned; in keeping them there is great reward" (Psalm 19:10–11).

PSALM 145:8

The LORD is gracious and compassionate, slow to anger and rich in love.

Recently I've been working on memorizing a portion of Psalm 145. The description of God in these verses is so encouraging, and I'm thankful that He is slow to anger and rich in love. Next week I'm going to have the opportunity of visiting the home of Henry Lyte in England. He wrote one of my favorite hymns, "Praise My Soul, the King of Heaven." The second verse describes God as "slow to chide, and swift to bless." During times of faults and failures, I go back to this biblical truth to find sweet and incredible reassurance.

PROVERBS 22:1

A good name is more desirable than great riches; to
be esteemed is better than silver or gold.

There's something else said to be worth possessing, the rich privilege of living a biblical life of personal holiness, character, and reputation. Even the poorest person on earth can do that. We can be rich in what others think of us. I began this chapter by talking about a man who had great riches but a repugnant reputation. I have met wealthy people who are gracious, generous, humble, and godly. But that takes incredible maturity. Jesus said that the wealth of this world can choke the Word of God in our lives and make us unfruitful. But whatever our financial status, we can build a reputation based on godliness and integrity. That is more desirable than great riches, and far better than silver or gold.

THE WEALTH OF THIS WORLD CAN CHOKE THE WORD OF GOD IN OUR LIVES.

PROVERBS 22:4

Humility is the fear of the LORD; its wages are riches and honor and life.

In his fascinating autobiography, *Just As I Am*, Billy Graham told of vacationing with his wife, Ruth, in the Caribbean. A rich man, age seventy-five, invited them to his lavish home for lunch. Nearly in tears, he told them, "I am the most miserable man in the world. Out there is my yacht. I can go anywhere I want to. I have my private plane, my helicopters. I have everything I want to make my life happy, yet I am as miserable as hell."

Later that day they met with a local Baptist pastor. Like the wealthy man, he was also seventy-five years old. He was a widower who cared for his two invalid sisters. He was full of enthusiasm and love for Christ and others. "I don't have two pounds to my name," he said with a smile, "but I am the happiest man on this island."

Afterward Billy asked Ruth, "Who do you think is the richer man?" She didn't have to reply because the answer was obvious.[3]

Never underestimate the unbelievable value of being a humble child of the King of kings.

Chapter 29

WHATEVER HAPPENS . . .

CONSIDER YOURSELF WORTH MILLIONS PART 2

(PHILIPPIANS 4:19)

I t was the best of times for Suleman Dawood, nineteen, a tall Pakistani university student in Scotland. He'd finished his first year in business school and was looking forward to summer. He came from a family of immense wealth. His every need was provided, yet it never seemed to go to his head. He was popular among his fellow students as he walked around campus with a Rubik's Cube in his hands and a smile on his face. He planned to work in the family business after graduating.

His father, Shahzada, with a net worth between $350 million and $400 million, was involved in business ventures across Europe and Asia. His career has been helped by his friendly face and incisive mind. In 2012, the World Economic Forum had named Shahzada a Young Global Leader. His hobby was photography, and he was close to his son.

The Dawood family had a lovely home in London, but they decided to spend a month in Canada during Suleman's summer break. Money was never a problem, and during this time father and son were inseparable. When Father's Day came, they embarked on a great adventure, one that unexpectedly thrust them into global headlines and worldwide alarm.

They descended to the depths of the Atlantic Ocean to see the ruins of the *Titanic*, and they never returned. They were among the five who perished when their small submarine imploded under the vast pressures of the watery deep, and their names were tragically added to the sad list of *Titanic* victims.

Money is not always our friend, and a simple lifestyle isn't a bad thing. People with vast wealth can be removed from their money in an instant. Life has a way of imploding for those who don't have eternal riches.

We're much healthier when we minimize the importance of wealth we cannot keep, and maximize our enjoyment of the wealth we cannot lose—the inheritance that's ours "according to the riches of his glory in Christ Jesus" (Philippians 4:19).

Let's continue looking at biblical passages that appraise our inheritance.

PROVERBS 28:20 AND ROMANS 10:12
A faithful person will be richly blessed. . . .

There is no difference between Jew and Gentile—the same
Lord is Lord of all and richly blesses all who call on him.

The Bible is full of the word "blessed," which conveys the idea of being in an enviable place in life, fortunate, happy, where we want to be, a place that provides rich internal enjoyment. But we aren't just blessed. We are *richly* blessed if we cultivate faithfulness to God and toward others in all things, large and small. Jew or Gentile, it doesn't matter. The Lord is faithful to us, and we can walk in the footsteps of His faithfulness.

EPHESIANS 2:4
God . . . is rich in mercy . . .

We also have the richness of God's mercy, which is a word that occurs in its various forms almost two hundred times in the Bible. It conveys God's sympathy and empathy for us when we create problems for ourselves. It's His compassion that moves Him to quickly forgive us whenever we confess our sins and return to Him. It's His charity that moves Him to meet our needs, untangle our problems, and give us the abundant life, which we don't deserve, but for Christ. He isn't stingy with His mercy. He bestows it richly.

You and I may never be worth a million dollars, but we're the recipients of a million blessings; we're part of a family of untold millions with whom we will share fellowship forever and ever; our eternal worth and net value is beyond contemplation; and when we've been there ten million years, bright shining as the sun, we've no less days to sing God's praise than when we first begun.

HE ISN'T STINGY WITH HIS MERCY. HE BESTOWS IT RICHLY.

ISAIAH 33:6

[The Lord] will be the sure foundation for your times, a rich store of salvation and wisdom and knowledge; the fear of the Lord is the key to this treasure.

Isaiah 33:6 is an answer to prayer. Isaiah had just asked, "Lord, be gracious to us; we long for you. Be our strength every morning, our salvation in time of distress" (v. 2). In response, Isaiah was told, "The Lord is exalted, for he dwells on high; he will fill Zion with his justice and righteousness" (v. 5).

Then we have this magnificent promise in verse 6: "He will be the sure foundation for your times."

In times like these, there is no other sure foundation. The world has never seen such times as these, when the international economy is a house of cards, the entire globe could be plunged into darkness by hackers, the leaders of the world are jockeying for power, pandemics could rage, weapons could detonate, and the events of the book of Revelation could unfold.

We cannot find a sturdy place to stand in our waffling circumstances. But the Lord Himself is a sure foundation. He is our Rock, and all other ground is sinking sand.

In Christ, He opens to us a rich storehouse of salvation. He doesn't just save us from the transience of earth; He doesn't simply take us to a remote corner of heaven. He opens all the storehouses of His wealth. He gives us the riches of growing in our knowledge of Him.

The fear of the Lord is the key to this treasure.

The reverent awe and respect for the majesty of our wonderful God is a key that unlocks all His riches for His children.

EPHESIANS 1:18

I pray that the eyes of your heart may be enlightened in order
that you may know the hope to which he has called you, the
riches of his glorious inheritance in his holy people.

The phrase "the eyes of your heart" is unusual. It's found nowhere in the Old Testament or in other Jewish literature. It is unique to Paul, but how descriptive. Just as our bodies have eyes that let us see all that's physical, our hearts have eyes that let us see all that's spiritual. Paul wanted us to have our full vision focused on the certain hope that awaits us in the future, to keep it in our line of sight.

But what of the phrase, "the riches of his glorious inheritance in his holy people"?

That is not something He has for us. It *is* us.

It is not our inheritance in Him. It is His inheritance of us.

Jesus Christ, who died for us in the cruelest of ways and who rose again, will bring to conclusion the entire drama of redemption, and we will forever be His people, His inheritance. To Him it is rich, something He values—being with you and me forever.

Dr. Andrew Lincoln, in his massive commentary on Ephesians, says about the phrase, "his inheritance":

"Here in 1:18 the talk is of . . . His inheritance, God's inheritance, which
focuses not so much on what He gives His people as on the other side . . . His
possession of His people. . . . Here it is God's inheritance which is in view and
His inheritance consists of the believers who now constitute His people. . . .

This part of the writer's petition, then, is that the readers might appreciate the wonder, the glory of what God has done in entering into possession of His people, the church, Jews and Gentiles, and the immense privilege it is to be among these saints."[1]

EPHESIANS 3:8

Although I am less than the least of all the Lord's people, this grace was given me: to preach to the Gentiles the boundless riches of Christ.

Jesus Christ and His gospel is the richest, wealthiest truth ever shared with humanity. But it's not just a matter of riches. It's a matter of *boundless* riches. In other words, the riches that come to those who respond to the gospel have no boundaries. They are infinite in all directions.

Do you know there is no such thing as an American $1,000 bill? American currency only comes in $1, $2, $5, $10, $20, $50, and $100. To give someone $1,000, you have to hand them ten $100 bills.

Last night, I gave a nice copy of the Bible to a man who is starting to awaken to His spiritual needs. If I had used $100 bills for bookmarks and put them between the pages, he would have been thrilled. I didn't do that, but I believe in time he's going to realize that the words on the pages—the gospel of Christ—are a message of boundless personal riches to him.

WHENEVER WE SHARE OUR FAITH WE ARE PREACHING THE BOUNDLESS RICHES OF CHRIST.

We seldom give people large sums of money, but whenever we share our faith we are preaching the boundless riches of Christ.

EPHESIANS 3:16

I pray that out of his glorious riches he may strengthen you with power through his Spirit in your inner being.

Sometimes I study the Bible by imagining what the verse would say without all its words. For example, Paul could have prayed that God would strengthen them with power. That would have been a wonderful prayer. But he added, "I pray out of his riches he may strengthen you with power." But not just riches, they are "glorious riches." And from those glorious riches power comes into our inner being, conveyed there by the Holy Spirit.

Personally, this is a prayer that I need to circle back to on a regular basis. Since COVID, I've battled fatigue. It's affected me physically, and the physical fatigue has affected me emotionally. Grief may have something to do with it, too, along with being in my eighth decade. But God's power comes from a very rich source—His own omnipotence. He runs a power line from His omnipotence to our need, and the Holy Spirit runs along the wire to empower us with optimism, with strength, and with all the energy we need to do what He has commanded, and to bear what He has allowed.

I am resting my full weight on this verse.

Make this a prayer for yourself. Offered right now. *Lord, out of Your glorious riches strengthen me with power through Your spirit and my innermost being.*

COLOSSIANS 1:27

To them God has chosen to make known among the Gentiles the glorious riches of this mystery, which is Christ in you, the hope of glory.

Paul evidently wrote Ephesians and Colossians at roughly the same time, because Colossians is modeled after Ephesians, though its purpose isn't just to relay glorious information but to challenge a growing heresy, which we call the Colossian heresy. In both books, Paul refered to the church as God's mystery, His secret, which the prophets didn't understand. Only in the early days of the book of Acts did the apostles gain insights about this new entity God was creating. Colossians 1:26 talks about "the mystery that has been kept hidden for ages and generations, but is now disclosed to the Lord's people."

God's secret plan was to establish the church of Jesus Christ, made up of both Jews and Gentiles, who would call Christ Messiah and be, on earth, "his body, which is the church" (v. 24).

This mystery is filled with "glorious riches," the greatest of all being "Christ in us." By the Holy Spirit of Jesus, our Lord indwells and fills His people, giving them the richest experience anyone could ever have on this planet.

Christ is among us. Christ is within us. He is within you by His indwelling Spirit, and that guarantees our future glorious eternal state.

It's helpful to remember this when you attend church this weekend. Yours isn't an ideal church; it has problems. So did the church in Colossae, in Philippi, and especially in Corinth. But the richness of our experience with our church doesn't depend on our human performance, but on His divine presence. He is walking among His lampstands (Revelation 1:12–13, 20).

COLOSSIANS 2:2
My goal is that they may be encouraged in heart and united
in love, so that they may have the full riches . . .

Here's another reference to our wealth in the book of Colossians. Paul was praying here for the believers in Colossae. This is his petition as rendered by the Living Bible: "that you will be encouraged and knit together by strong ties of love, and that you will have the rich experience of knowing Christ with real certainty and clear understanding."

I think my favorite book outside of the Bible is J. I. Packer's *Knowing God*. In this classic work, Packer says:

How can we turn our knowledge about God into knowledge of God? The rule for doing so is simple but demanding. It is that we turn each truth that we learn about God into a matter of meditation before God, leading to prayer and praise to God.

He went on to say that the effect of doing so "is ever to humble us, as we contemplate God's greatness and glory and our own littleness and sinfulness, and to encourage and reassure us—comfort us, in the old, strong, Bible sense of the word—as we contemplate the unsearchable riches of divine mercy displayed and the Lord Jesus Christ."[2]

The unsearchable, inexhaustible, incalculable richness of knowing Him, personally, intimately, eternally—that is the very best thing in life.

COLOSSIANS 3:16
Let the message of Christ dwell among you richly.

The older translations say, "Let the word of God dwell in you richly." That sounds like an individual instruction for each of us to become saturated with the Word of God. The above translation recognizes the fact that the "you" is plural, and that Paul is saying the entire church should be saturated with the Word of God.

Of course, both are true.

I fell in love with the Bible almost as soon as I learned to read. I got a small Gospel of John for learning the Twenty-third Psalm, and I remember my father buying me a small New Testament with olive wood covers. Soon thereafter, I received a copy of the entire Bible. In those days the King James Version was the dominant translation, but because I heard it read in Sunday school and church I was able to navigate through the archaic terms. My local elementary school had scripture memory exercises, and I memorized a ton of Bible verses.

In high school my father bought me a very nice Bible, leather bound, ribbons, tabs, and I read it every day.

At Columbia International University, my knowledge of the Bible grew exponentially, and I began learning to teach it and preach it to others. It has been the book of my life. The more I study it the more I want to study it. As I can lay it on the table in front of me, God lays its words on my heart. My very favorite thing to do in all of this life is to study God's Word and to teach it to others, however feeble my efforts.

This wonderful book has sustained me through childhood, adolescence, young adulthood, marriage and parenting, and widowership, and it will bear me through to the very end. And when I rise in glory and see the face of our Lord Jesus and hug my wife, Katrina, and my dear parents, the next thing I want to do is to open a copy of the Bible in heaven and begin studying it all over again. Forever is His word settled in heaven (see Psalm 119:89).

2 PETER 1:11
And you will receive a rich welcome into the eternal
kingdom of our Lord and Savior Jesus Christ.

All of that brings us to the next verse, about receiving a rich welcome into the eternal kingdom of Jesus our Lord and Savior. Verse 10 tells us to make certain we are among those called by God and committed to Jesus Christ, which can keep us from stumbling. If we do that, we can be assured of a rich welcome when we enter heaven.

What is a rich welcome?

You won't have to sneak into heaven, like Joshua's two spies sneaked into Jericho. You won't enter unnoticed and alone, as Paul entered Athens. You won't have to be worried or apprehensive like Jacob when he returned home to face his brother. You won't face rejection, as Jesus did in His hometown synagogue.

Instead, you will be richly welcomed, with shouts and songs and splendor. Friends will be there from long ago. Generations will be lined up to meet you. Angels will greet you. Your mansion will be prepared for you. The Lord will be there waiting. You won't just get into heaven, you will be *richly* welcomed into your heavenly home.

When the poor beggar died in Luke 16, he was carried by the angels to be with Abraham and all the Old Testament heroes. When Stephen died in Acts 6, the Lord stood up to welcome him. When Paul was transported to the third heaven, he saw and heard things so resplendent in beauty that he could not repeat them later. When John was caught up into heaven in Revelation 4, he was thrilled at the worship occurring around the throne.

YOU WON'T JUST GET INTO HEAVEN, YOU WILL BE *RICHLY* WELCOMED.

One Sunday afternoon, Charles Spurgeon was preaching about the New Jerusalem. A woman sat near the front on the right side of the room. He noticed how her eyes sparkled as he preached, and there was a look of sheer joy on her face.

He kept preaching about the riches of our heavenly home, and he glanced down at her again. This time she appeared nonresponsive. He stopped his sermon and said, "I think that sister is dead." And she was.

(I can relate to that. Once when I was preaching, I sensed that a woman had died during my sermon. I stopped the message and we called for medical help. She wasn't dead, but she passed away shortly afterward.)

In Spurgeon's case, the woman had literally gone home while he was describing it to her.

In talking about the experience later, he said, "We may go to sleep tonight, and awake in eternal glory. We are not far from home; so let us be of good cheer, and rejoice, and praise and bless our Divine Lord that ever He should have stooped so low to raise us so high."[3]

Jesus came all the way to earth to prepare a way for you to be with Him forever, and He has been waiting for two thousand years for your arrival. It will be a rich welcome.

That's a fitting reason to let our last verse be a doxology of praise, as found in Romans 11:33:

> Oh, the depth of the riches of the wisdom and knowledge of God!
>
> How unsearchable his judgments, and his paths beyond tracing out!

Chapter 30

WHATEVER HAPPENS . . .

BEGIN AND END EVERYTHING WITH PRAYER AND PRAISE

(PHILIPPIANS 4:21-23)

Years ago I was speaking at the Billy Graham Training Center at The Cove in Asheville, North Carlina. Cliff Barrows approached me and asked about my subject. I told him I was going to speak from Psalm 92. Cliff immediately began quoting it from the Living Bible. He quoted the entire psalm word for word.

I can still hear his friendly, lilting voice as he began, "It is good to say thank you to the Lord, to sing praises to the God who is above all gods. Every morning tell him, 'Thank you for your kindness,' and every evening rejoice in all his faithfulness" (TLB).

We should begin and end our lives with praise and prayer—every day we live, everything we do, every trip we take, every burden we bear. When we wrap up everything with prayer and praise, it's less likely to come unraveled. Let us thank Him for His kindness and rejoice in all His faithfulness.

The ending of the letter to the Philippians brings the epistle full circle,

WE SHOULD BEGIN AND END OUR LIVES WITH PRAISE AND PRAYER.

concluding with Paul's final greetings and benediction. He opened with prayer in chapter 1, and he ends that way with this final paragraph:

Greet all God's people in Christ Jesus. The brothers and sisters who are with me send greetings. All God's people here send you greetings, especially those who belong to Caesar's household. The grace of the Lord Jesus Christ be with your spirit. Amen. (Philippians 4:21–23)

Paul's mention of Caesar's household was undoubtedly intended to encourage the Philippians that people within Nero's own circle were being converted. The word "household" here isn't necessarily limited to his family; it would include his staff of servants and even his bodyguard, the Pretorian Guard that had been guarding Paul. He was telling them that despite his imprisonment and regardless of the persecution that was taking place, the gospel was expanding.

He then concluded his book with the benediction: "The grace of the Lord Jesus Christ be with your spirit. Amen."

As I mentioned earlier in the book, as a senior pastor, I loved being able to pray the benediction over my congregation at the end of our Lord's Day services. This is a biblical technique, going all the way back to the priestly benediction of Numbers chapter 6.

Throughout the Bible, benedictions (Latin: good diction, or good words, or blessings) were used to summarize how God wanted to bless His people. Finding the benedictions of the Bible, using them in worship services, and praying them for yourself and others is at the heart of developing an effective pattern of prayer.

Sometimes these benedictions are preceded by the word "may," but other times the "may" is unstated but understood.

There is a question whether benedictions are prayers or pronouncements. Liturgists have debated this question for ages. Am I praying the benediction or pronouncing the benediction? It sounds like a prayer, yet it is addressed not to God, but to the people.

I call it a very special species of prayer. Pronouncing a benediction over His disciples was our Lord's last action as He was ascending to heaven (Luke 24:50–53). I encourage you to search out and use the benedictions of the Bible as you pray for your children, grandchildren, husband or wife, friends, and family, and any others whom the Lord brings to your mind.

Begin and end everything that you do—and every day you live—with prayer and praise.

And to you, I say:

The grace of the Lord Jesus Christ be with your spirit. Amen.

Chapter 31

WHATEVER HAPPENS . . .

HANG ON TO THIS BOOK

(PHILIPPIANS—FINAL OVERVIEW)

This final chapter is a sort of appendix for those who want to better understand the way I have divided up this book of Philippians. I have a deep conviction that God gave us a unified Bible with a single story, but made up of sixty-six installments, which we call "books." Each one of these sixty-six books has its own unique message for us. It's as though the Lord recognizes that we have sixty-six spiritual needs within us, and He has given us a book in the Bible to meet each need.

Just as every book has its own purpose, so each has its own background, context, and unfolding plan. I believe in preaching through books of the Bible as a primary pastoral method of preaching, because in doing so we are able to trace the unfolding logic that represents God's thinking, which is embedded in each book.

Paul had entered the city of Philippi—its population estimated at ten thousand to fifteen thousand—about the year AD 50 on his second missionary tour. The story is told in Acts 16, where we meet the first converts who made up the charter membership of the church. It's unclear how long he was able to stay in the city, but when he was forced out, Luke stayed behind. It's undoubtedly because of Paul's leadership that the Philippian church became so strong and generous. He organized the church very well with its elders and deacons (Philippians 1:1).

Eight years later, Paul was able to visit again (Acts 20:3), and in the year AD 62 Paul wrote this letter to them from Rome, where he was imprisoned.

It was not only Paul's letter to the Philippians; it is God's letter to us. No one can study it too much or memorize too many of its verses. It can be easily read in ten minutes, but it takes a lifetime to absorb the richness of its simple teaching.

I'm convinced the first twenty-six verses of Philippians are introductory, in which Paul primarily gave his friends an update, with an encouraging spin, about his circumstances.

IT WAS NOT ONLY PAUL'S LETTER TO THE PHILIPPIANS; IT IS GOD'S LETTER TO US.

The internal body of the letter runs from 1:27 to 4:1.

The final twenty-two verses, Philippians 4:2 through 4:23, is an extended conclusion in which Paul talked about the Philippians and the implications of their gift to him, again with encouraging twists at every point.

The theme of the letter is stated in 1:27–28:

> Whatever happens, conduct yourselves in a manner worthy of the gospel of Christ. Then, whether I come and see you or only hear about you in my absence, I will know that you stand firm in the one Spirit, striving together as one for the faith of the gospel without being frightened in any way by those who oppose you.

In the main corpus, or body, of his letter, Paul unpacked his theme by giving us a glorious theological statement about Jesus Christ, with its practical implications; by holding up the examples of Timothy and Epaphroditus; and by presenting himself as a model.

He wrapped up the central message of the book by saying, "Therefore, my brothers and sisters . . . stand firm in the Lord in this way, dear friends!" (4:1).

The topic of joy is an uplifting subtheme of this book, and all the way through we're exposed to uplifting exhortations to humility, love, and oneness.

The following graphic is offered as a visual to help you see the book of Philippians at a glance.

Philippians

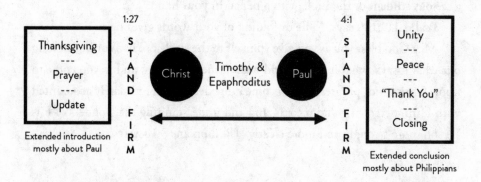

Key Verse

Whatever happens, conduct yourselves in a manner worth of the gospel of Christ. Then, whether I come and see you or only hear about you in my absence, I will know that you stand firm in one Spirit, striving together as one for the faith of the gospel.

Philippians 1:27

Purpose

Whatever happens, we must stand firm in Christ, united and joyful.

Notes

- Philippians is Paul's most personal church letter. He established the church in Acts 16 with his own blood, and the Philippian Christians were devoted to him, sending him financial help more than once.

- This letter was written during Paul's Roman imprisonment (Acts 28), when the Philippians had sent a gift by the hand of Epaphroditus, who had gone to attend to Paul's needs (Philippians 2:25–30).

- Paul apparently learned from Epaphroditus of some church distress and disunity in the face of persecution, so he encouraged them to stand firm and united.

- The concept of joy occurs sixteen times in this letter. One writer called it "a spiritual tonic, fitted to brace one up when he is low in spirits."

237

I want to encourage you, as you read the Bible, to look for divisions, obvious sections, and themes. You don't have to be a great theological scholar, just a serious student of the Bible with a pencil in your hand.

Psalm 119:130 says, "The unfolding of your words gives light."

May God bless you as you give yourself to the study of His Word, searching out what it says, what it means, and what it means to you; and as you come to know Christ and "progressively become more deeply and intimately acquainted with Him, perceiving and recognizing and understanding the wonders of His Person more strongly and more clearly" (Philippians 3:10 AMPC).

ACKNOWLEDGMENTS

My deepest thanks goes to my assistant, Sherry Anderson, who has worked by my side for decades, proofing sermons, reviewing chapters, planning flights, writing checks, guarding privacy, answering calls, giving advice, and making everything better than it was before it crossed her desk.

Luke Tyler, to whom this book is dedicated, started this project as my intern and ended it as my grandson-in-law. He's the best! Luke also wrote the study guide for Whatever Happens.

Matt and Sealy Yates, my literary agents, have been a God-sent team, helping me for many years. I cherish their partnership and friendship.

The galaxy of talent at W Publishing has amazed me. Kyle Olund has been a senior editor on my projects since The Red Sea Rules in 2001. Rachel Buller is an incredible editor who knows my voice but makes it better. And how can I adequately thank Allison Carter and Kerri Daly for their expertise in publicity and marketing? Any publishing house on the planet would want this team!

Brandon Riesgo provided the drawings within these pages. He's so intuitive at what he does, and he always picks up the phone when I call. Thank you, Brandon!

Casey Pontious is in charge of acquiring all the permissions for all my books, combing footnotes and making sure we're properly acknowledging everyone and everything. It takes a great burden off my shoulders.

Finally, thank you Joshua Rowe for your double help—with author-based marketing through Clearly Media, and with navigating biblical software through MP Seminars. Plus, you alone are able to advise me as you alone can.

And thank you, dear reader! As my father would say, "I'm much obliged!" May God bless you . . . whatever happens!

NOTES

Introduction

1. Eliza Goren, Shefali S. Kulkarni, and Kanyakrit Vongkiatkajorn, "The Washington Post Asked Readers to Describe 2020," *Washington Post*, December 8, 2020, https://www.washingtonpost.com/graphics/2020/lifestyle/2020-in-one-word/.

Chapter 1: Whatever Happens . . . Trust God's Guidance When Perplexed

1. John Mack Faragher, *Daniel Boone*, (New York: Henry Holt and Company, 1992), 65.
2. William M. Ramsay, *St. Paul the Traveler and the Roman Citizen*, (Grand Rapids: Baker Book House, 1982), 198.
3. Greg Hinnant, *Philippian Notes*, (Lake Mary, FL: Creation House, 2015), xvi: "Hosting a medical school, Philippi may have been Luke's hometown or possibly the site where he studied medicine prior to joining Paul on the latter's second missionary journey."
4. Robert Morgan, *Then Sings My Soul* (Nashville: Thomas Nelson Publishers, 2003), 145.
5. J. H. Gilmore, "He Leadeth Me," 1862.

Chapter 2: Whatever Happens . . . Build Your Own Mental Hymnbook

1. Matthew Harmon, *Philippians*, (Fearn, Tain, Ross-shire, Scotland: Christian Focus Publications, 2015), 26.
2. Petr Jasek, *Imprisoned with ISIS*, (Washington, DC: Regnery: Salem Books, 2020), 124.
3. Daniel Silliman, "We've No Less Days to Sing God's Praise, But New Worship Songs Only Last a Few Years," *Christianity Today*, November 22, 2021, https://

www.christianitytoday.com/ct/2021/december/worship–music–lifespan–shrinking
–faster–study–tanner–ccli.html.

4. Based on a personal conversation with Bill Welte.

5. Charles Wesley, "O For a Thousand Tongues to Sing," 1739.

Chapter 3: Whatever Happens . . . Layer Your Life with Generosity

1. Warner Davis, "He Learned a Valuable Lesson About Tithing and Faith," *Guideposts*, June 24, 2022, https://guideposts.org/angels-and-miracles/angels/he-learned-a-valuable-lesson-about-tithing-and-faith/.

2. Matthew Harmon, *Philippians*, (Fearn, Tain, Ross-shire, Scotland: Christian Focus Publications, 2015), 42.

3. Rob Moll, "Want More Growth in China? Have Faith," *Wall Street Journal*, August 8, 2008, at https://www.wsj.com/articles/SB121815556386722667.

4. Moll, "Want More Growth in China?"

5. Chuck Bentley, "The Priceless Economic Impact of Bible Believing Churches," *Patheos*, May 26, 2020, https://www.crown.org/blog/the–priceless–economic–impact–of–bible–believing–churches/.

Chapter 4: Whatever Happens . . . Rely on Revitalizing Grace

1. O. Procksch and K. G. Kuhn. (1964–). ἅγιος–ἁγιάζω–ἁγιασμός ἁγιότης–ἁγιωσύνη, in G. Kittel, G. W. Bromiley, & G. Friedrich (Eds.), *Theological Dictionary of the New Testament* (electronic ed., Vol. 1, p. 88). Eerdmans.

2. Wikipedia entry on "Edward Crozier Creasy," sourced from "British Pluck Foils Poles Who Had Orders to Shoot," *Ottawa Citizen*, Ontario, Canada, May 28, 1921, 15.

3. David Allen, *The New American Commentary: Hebrews*, (Nashville: B&H, 2010), 503.

4. 1 Corinthians 7:21.

5. Romans 6:22.

6. Andrew Murray, *Humility and Absolute Surrender*, (Peabody, MA: Hendrickson Publishers, 2005), 2.

7. Annie J. Flint, "He Giveth More Grace," copyright 1941, renewed by Lillenas in 1969.

Chapter 5: Whatever Happens . . . Remember God Is Still Working on You

1. William Le Roy Stidger, *More Sermons in Stories*, (New York: Abingdon-Cokesbury Press, 1944), 118.

2. George Herbert, *The Poems of George Herbert*, (London: Oxford University Press, 1907), 111.

3. Frank Laubach, *Prayer: The Mightiest Force in the World*, (Burtyrki Books, 2020), 12 and passim.

4. Ray Ortlund, "Have You Said This to Your Son?" *Gospel Coalition* (blog), December 16, 2012, https://www.thegospelcoalition.org/blogs/ray-ortlund /have-you-said-this-yet-to-your-son/.

5. Words by Joel Hemphill.

6. William Hendrickson, *Philippians, Colossians, and Philemon*, (Grand Rapids: Baker, 1979), 55.

Chapter 6: Whatever Happens . . . Invigorate Your Life Through Prayer

1. Laura Neutzling, "Tim Tebow," *Jesus Calling* magazine, Summer 2022, 9.

2. "Kylie Jenks Sentenced to Maximum for Role in Deadly Fire," WLKY, last updated October 17, 2014, https://www.wlky.com/article/kylie-jenks-sentenced -to-maximum-for-role-in-deadly-fire/3753099#.

3. B. Mansell Ramsey, "Teach Me Thy Way," published in 1919.

4. J. I. Packer, *Rediscovering Holiness*, (Grand Rapids: Baker Book House, 2009), 17.

5. Major Ian Thomas, *The Indwelling Life of Christ*, (Colorado Springs: Multnomah Books, 2006), 101.

6. "Sculptor Gutzon Borglum," National Park Service, last updated January 25, 2023, https://www.nps.gov/moru/learn/historyculture/gutzon-borglum.htm.

7. Randy Alcorn, *The Grace and Truth Paradox*, (Colorado Springs: Multnomah Books, 2003), 14.

Chapter 7: Whatever Happens . . . Replace Gloomy Thoughts with Glorious Ones

1. Robert J. Morgan, *God Works All Things Together for Your Good*, (Robert J. Morgan, 2020), xi–xii.

2. Daniel Hofkamp, "God Is Glorified Even in the Midst of Ukraine's Darkest Hours," *Evangelical Focus*, July 21, 2022, https://evangelicalfocus.com/europe /17857/god-is-glorified-even-in-the-midst-of-ukraine-darkest-hours.

Chapter 8: Whatever Happens . . . Access God's Provision of the Spirit of Christ

1. *Joy Starts Here*, ed. Dr. E. James Wilder III et al. (Independently Published, 2013).

2. Eileen Crossman, *Mountain Rain: A New Biography of James O. Fraser*, (Singapore: OMF Books, 1982), 17.

3. "The Prayer of Faith" at https://www.path2prayer.com/prevailing–intercessory –prayer/what–is–the–prayer–of–faith/james–fraser–the–prayer–of–faith.

4. B. B. McKinney, "Send a Great Revival," public domain.

5. From my notes based on Major Ian Thomas's sermon "The Baptism of the Holy Spirit."

6. Major Ian Thomas, *The Indwelling Life of Christ*, (Colorado Springs: Multnomah Books, 2006), 64.

7. From my notes based on Major Ian Thomas' Sermon "The Baptism of the Holy Spirit."

Chapter 9: Whatever Happens . . . Choose a Life Motto

1. Orison Swett Marden, *Everybody Ahead: Or, Getting the Most Out of Life*, (New York: Frank E. Morrison Publisher, 1916), 310–312.

2. Karen Ruth Johnson, "My Philosophy of Life," June 4, 1959, via Messages of God's Love (BibleTruth, 1979), https://bibletruthpublishers.com/karen-ruth -johnson/messages-of-gods-love-1979/la176578.

3. Based on a personal conversation with Betty Byrd on August 31, 2022. Also see https://cityonahillstudio.com/bettys-story-gods-grace-greater-tragedy/ and https://teamexpansion.org/resilience-in-the-view-of-danger/.

Chapter 10: Whatever Happens . . . Never Be Intimidated

1. "A Church in Exile," *The Voice of the Martyrs*, September 2022, Vol. 56, No. 9: 7–9.

2. Gordon D. Fee, *The New International Commentary on the New Testament: Paul's Letter to the Philippians*, (Grand Rapids: Eerdmans, 1995), 159.

3. Andrew Brunson, *God's Hostage* (Grand Rapids: Baker Books, 2019), 208.

Chapter 11: Whatever Happens . . . Make Today About Others

1. Gordon D. Fee, *The New International Commentary on the New Testament: Paul's Letter to the Philippians*, (Grand Rapids: Eerdmans, 1995), 180–181.

2. Earl B. Russell, *Cold Turkey at Nine*, (Bloomington, IN: iUniverse, 2013), 27.

3. John Newton, "May the Grace of Christ Our Savior," 1779.

Chapter 12: Whatever Happens . . . Cultivate the Mind of Christ

1. Charles Wesley, "And Can It Be, That I Should Gain," 1738.

2. Richard Walkden, "Politician Crucifies Himself After Staging Hunger Strike in Extreme Protest at Election Snub," *The Mirror*, January 23, 2015, https://www

.mirror.co.uk/news/world-news/politician-crucifies-himself-after-staging -5029675.

3. Dr. Harold J. Sala, "What Seminary Can't Teach," Guidelines for Living.

Chapter 13: Whatever Happens . . . Work Out What God Works In

1. John Piper, "God Is Always Doing 10,000 Things in Your Life," *Desiring God* (blog), January 1, 2013, https://www.desiringgod.org/articles/god-is-always -doing-10000-things-in-your-life.

2. Charles Haddon Spurgeon, "Working Out What Is Worked In," Metropolitan Tabernacle Pulpit Volume 14, July 12, 1868, https://www.spurgeon.org /resource-library/sermons/working-out-what-is-worked-in/#flipbook/.

3. Warren W. Wiersbe, *Be Joyful*, (Colorado Springs: David C. Cook, 1974), 81.

4. Jesse L. Holman (words), Thomas A. Arne (music), "Lord, in Thy presence here we meet," 1762, in Absalom Graves, Hymns, Psalms, and Spiritual Songs, 2nd ed., no. 263, 1829, http://www.hymntime.com/tch/htm/l/o/r/d/i/lordithy.htm.

Chapter 14: Whatever Happens . . . Shine Like a Star in the Blackened Sky

1. "What Is Olbers' Paradox?" National Aeronautics and Space Administration, Goddard Space Flight Center, https://lambda.gsfc.nasa.gov/product/suborbit /POLAR/cmb.physics.wisc.edu/tutorial/olbers.html.

2. Gordon Fee, *The New International Commentary on the New Testament: Paul's Letter to the Philippians*, (Grand Rapids: Eerdmans, 1995), 241–242.

3. Orison Swett Marden, *The Joys of Living*, (New York: Thomas Y. Crowell Company, 1913), 237–238.

4. Marden, 38.

5. Kate B. Wilkinson, "May the Mind of Christ, My Savior," 1925.

6. Timothy Keller (@timkellernyc), 2018, "If you met a truly humble person, you wouldn't think him/her humble, but happy and incredibly interested in you," Twitter, August 23, 2018, 1:39 p.m., https://twitter.com/timkellernyc/status /1032698743244636160.

7. Adapted from Marden, 14–15.

8. Dave Crampton, "Australian Football Executive Forced to Resign, Prompting Debate about Religious Liberty," *Christianity Today*, October 14, 2022, https:// www.christianitytoday.com/news/2022/october/andrew-thorburn-essendon -resign-discrimination-lgbt.html.

9. Personal conversation with Jeff Brigstock on October 20, 2022.

Chapter 15: Whatever Happens . . . Stay as Cheerful as Possible in all Circumstances

1. Robert J. Morgan, *Worry Less, Live More,* (Nashville: W Publishing Group, 2017), 55.
2. Layne Saliba, "For Julie Chapman, Beating Cancer Came Down to Faith, Family and Sticky Notes," *Gainesville Time*s, June 22, 2019, https://www.forsythnews.com/local/julie–chapman–beating–cancer–came–down–faith–family–and–sticky–notes/.
3. Krystal Whitten, *Faith and Lettering,* (Nashville: Worthy, 2019), adapted from the introduction.
4. Michael Parsons, "'In Christ' in Paul," *Vox Evangelica*, 18 (1988): 25–44.

Chapter 16: Whatever Happens . . . Never Think of Quitting

1. Leah Adler, "Footsteps of My Father: A Story of Courage, Resilience, and Honor," Jewish Standard, November 2, 2022, https://jewishstandard.timesofisrael.com/footsteps-of-my-father-a-story-of-courage-resilience-and-honor/.
2. Technically there are two nations that don't allow Coca-Cola: North Korea and Cuba. But even there, you can find a Coke if you have to.
3. Gordon D. Fee, *Paul's Letter to the Philippians*, (Grand Rapids: Eerdmans, 1995), 275.
4. Bill Gilbert, *Ship of Miracles*, (Chicago: Triumph Books, 2000), 124.

Chapter 18: Whatever Happens . . . Value Christ Over Commas

1. Juliana Kaplan, "Heiress Abigail Disney says 'Billionaires are miserable, unhappy people,' and it's time for change: 'The billionaire bashing needs to happen. I don't know why we're being so polite'," Business Insider, April 12, 2022, https://www.businessinsider.com/abigail-disney-patriotic-millionaires-billionaires-miserable-unhappy-people-wealth-tax-2022-4.
2. S. M. Krager, "Judaizers," *The Lexham Bible Dictionary*, J. D. Barry et al., eds. (Lexham Press, 2016).
3. Roland Bainton, *Here I Stand: A Life of Martin Luther,* (Nashville: Abingdon-Cokesbury Press), 45.
4. Leah MarieAnn Klett, "Over Half of Christians Believe Good Works Will Get Them into Heaven: Study," *Christian Post*, August 11, 2020, https://www.christianpost.com/news/over-half-of-us-christians-believe-good-works-will-get-them-into-heaven-study.html.
5. Charles Haddon Spurgeon, *C. H. Spurgeon's Autobiography: The Life of the Great*

Baptist Preacher, https://www.amazon.com/C-H-Spurgeon-Autobiography-1834
-1859/dp/0851510760.

6. Caleb Parke, "Singapore's Richest Man Says 'Missing Piece was God through Jesus Christ'," Fox News, July 24, 2019, https://www.foxnews.com/faith-values /richest-man-singapore-god-jesus-wealth.

7. Rhea F. Miller, "I'd Rather Have Jesus," 1922.

Chapter 19: Whatever Happens . . . Grow Deeper Each Morning

1. Lisa Gray, "Finding Tamayo Painting Was Result of Fate," *Houston Chronicle*, November 2, 2007, https://www.chron.com/entertainment/article/Finding -Tamayo-painting-was-result-of-fate-1560737.php.

2. Graham Kendrick, "Knowing You (All I Once Held Dear)," (c) 1993 Make Way Music, www.grahamkendrick.co.uk.

3. Interview with Sam Rohrer on January 9, 2023.

4. George Bennard, "The Old Rugged Cross," 1913.

5. "Epiphany, Orthodoxy, and Seeing Christ All Year," an interview with Frederica Mathewes-Green on "Upstream" with Shane Morris, January 3, 2023.

Chapter 20: Whatever Happens . . . Actively Press On

1. Meb Keflezighi, *26 Marathons*, (New York: Rodale, 2019), 102–103.

2. Jeff Pack, *Witness to History: The Story of the Gideons International*, (Nashville, The Gideons International, 2018), 224.

3. Sabrina Talbert, Safire R. Sostre, and Lindsay Geller, "260 (Not Boring) Questions to Ask to Get to Know Someone Better," *Women's Health*, last updated November 7, 2023, https://www.womenshealthmag.com/life/a22500573 /questions-to-ask-to-get-to-know-someone/.

4. Marissa Postell Sullivan, "Churchgoers Value Time Alone with God, Practice Varies," Baptist Press, January 3, 2023, https://www.baptistpress.com/resource -library/news/churchgoers-value-time-alone-with-god-practice-varies/.

5. Gordon Fee, *God's Empowering Presence*, (Peabody, MA: Hendrickson Publishers, 1994), 14.

Chapter 21: Whatever Happens . . . Be Careful Who You Admire

1. From my notes of one of his sermons.

2. Chapter 1, verses 6, 10, 20, 21, 23. Chapter 2, verses 10–11, 16. Chapter 3, verses 11, 13–14, 20–21. Chapter 4, verses 1, 5.

Chapter 22: Whatever Happens . . . Project Yourself into the Future

1. The last word of the verse is my own paraphrase. The NIV uses the word "wasteland."

2. Samuel Dunn, *The Glorified Body: A Sermon Preached in the South–Parade Chapel, Halifax, on Sunday, October 16, 1842*, (London: J. Mason, 1842), passim.

3. The last word of the verse is my own paraphrase. The NIV uses the word "wasteland."

Chapter 23: Whatever Happens . . . Stand Firm

1. Matthew Harmon, *Philippians*, (Fearn, Tain, Ross-shire, Scotland: Christian Focus Publications, 2015393.

2. Saint Ignatius of Antioch (30–107), "Epistle to Polycarp," trans. Alexander Roberts and James Donaldson, Ch. 3, http://www.logoslibrary.org/ignatiu /polycarp2/3.html.

3. Nolan Rice Best, "Christian Endeavor," *The Interior* XXXVI, no. 1824 (May 11, 1905): 589.

4. Jonathan Edwards, *The Works of President Edwards: Volume IV*, (New York: Leavitt & Allen, 1852), 360.

5. Billy Graham, "Ambassadors for Christ: Stand Firm," BGEA, March 9, 2011, https://billygraham.org/story/ambassadors-for-christ-stand-firm/.

6. Amanda Casanova, "Christians Who 'Heavily Engage' with the Bible 'Flourish in Every Doman,' Study Finds," ChristianHeadlines.com, last updated June 14, 2023, https://www.christianheadlines.com/contributors/amanda-casanova/christians -who-heavily-engage-with-the-bible-flourish-in-every-domain-study-find.html.

7. Milton Quintanilla, "Christian Substitute Teacher Fired for Opposing Same-Sex Book Is Reinstated," ChristianHeadlines.com, last updated May 1, 2023, https://www.christianheadlines.com/contributors/milton-quintanilla/christian -substitute-teacher-fired-for-opposing-same-sex-book-is-reinstated.html.

Chapter 24: Whatever Happens . . . Have a Strategy for Imperfect Situations

1. Robert J. Morgan, *Then Sings My Soul*, (Nashville: Thomas Nelson, 2003), 264.

2. Edith L. Blumhoffer and Mark A. Noll, eds. *Singing the Lord's Song in a Strange Land*, (Tuscaloosa, AL: The University of Alabama Press, 2004), 234.

3. James W. Moore, *Attitude Is Your Paintbrush: It Colors Every Situation*, (Nashville: Abingdon, 1998), 9–10.

Chapter 25: Whatever Happens . . . Improve Your Mental Chemistry

1. Daniel G. Amen, *Change Your Brain Every Day*, (Carol Stream, IL: Tyndale House, 2023), 1.

2. Amen, *Change Your Brain Every Day*, 285.

3. Amen, 119.

4. Amen, 31.

5. Amen, 119.

6. Amen, 227.

7. William Barclay, *The Letters to the Philippians, Colossians, and Thessalonians*, (Philadelphia: Westminster Press, 1975), 79.

8. Annette Coffey, "Nuggets of Truth in Scripture," Then She Spoke: Encouraging Reflections by Annette (blog), September 27, 2021, https://thenshespoke.com /2021/09/.

9. Edmund Calamy, *The Art of Divine Meditation*, (Crossville, TN: Puritan Publications, 2019), 47.

10. Gordon F. Sander, "America Was Obsessed with This Self-Help Craze 100 Years Ago," *Washington Post*, March 13, 2023, https://www.washingtonpost .com/history/2023/03/13/emile-coue-autosuggestion-craze/.

Chapter 26: Whatever Happens . . . Discover the Secret to Contentment

1. Erik Raymond, *Chasing Contentment*, (Wheaton, IL: Crossway, 2017), 22.

2. J. H. Gilmore, "He Leadeth Me," 1862.

Chapter 27: Whatever Happens . . . Trust God with Every Single Need

1. "Bernard Arnault & Family," Forbes Profile, accessed December 7, 2023, https:// www.forbes.com/profile/bernard-arnault/?listuri=rtb&sh=465b26a166fa.

2. Matthew Harmon, *Philippians*, (Fearn, Tain, Ross-shire, Scotland: Christian Focus Publications, 2015), 42.

3. Gordon Fee, *The New International Commentary on the New Testament: Paul's Letter to the Philippians*, (Grand Rapids: Eerdmans, 1995), 252–253.

4. Adapted from Terry Powell and Mark Smith, *Oh God, I'm Dying!: How God Redeems Pain for Our Good and His Glory* (New York: Morgan James Faith, 2020).

5. Elizabeth Spiers, "My Husband Is About to Find Out Just How Rich I Am," Slate.com, June 30, 2022, https://slate.com/business/2022/06/inherit-millions -husband-unaware-advice.html.

Chapter 28: Whatever Happens . . . Consider Yourself Worth Millions Part 1

1. Melissa Nason Ferreura, "These People Inherited Fortunes—Then Blew Them All Away," GOBankingRates, February 17, 2021, https://www.gobankingrates .com/net-worth/debt/people-inherited-fortunes-then-blew-away/.

2. Charles Spurgeon, "Christ's Poverty, Our Riches," April 18, 1880, at https://www .spurgeon.org/resource–library/sermons/christs–poverty–our–riches/#flipbook/.

3. Billy Graham, *Just As I Am*, (HarperSanFrancisco/Zondervan, 1997), 697.

Chapter 29: Whatever Happens . . . Consider Yourself Worth Millions Part 2

1. Andrew T. Lincoln, *Word Bible Commentary: Ephesians* (Dallas: Word Books, 1990), 59–60.
2. J. I. Packer, *Knowing God*, IVP Signature Collection (1973; Westmont, IL: IVP, 2023).
3. Charles Spurgeon, "Christ's Poverty, Our Riches" April 18, 1880, https://www .spurgeon.org/resource–library/sermons/christs-poverty-our-riches/#flipbook/

ABOUT THE AUTHOR

Robert J. Morgan is a Bible teacher and podcaster who serves as associate pastor at World Outreach Chirch in Murfreesboro, Tennessee. He is the author of *The 50 Final Events in World History, 100 Bible Verses That Made America, The Strength You Need, Then Sings My Soul, The Red Sea Rules,* and many other titles, with approximately five million copies of his books in circulation. Contact him at robertjmorgan.com.

Rob is also a homemaker and was the caregiver for his late wife of forty-three years, Katrina, who battled multiple sclerosis and passed away in November of 2019. He and Katrina have three daughters and sixteen grandchildren.